Collins

KS3
Geography
Workbook

Janet Hutson and Dan Major

Revision Tips

Rethink Revision

Have you ever taken part in a quiz and thought '*I know this*!', but no matter how hard you scrabbled around in your brain you just couldn't come up with the answer?

It's very frustrating when this happens, but in a fun situation it doesn't really matter. However, in tests and assessments, it is essential that you can recall the relevant information when you need to.

Most students think that revision is about making sure you **know** *stuff*, but it is also about being confident that you can **retain** that *stuff* over time and **recall** it when needed.

Revision that Really Works

Experts have found that there are two techniques that help with *all* of these things and consistently produce better results in tests and exams compared to other revision techniques.

Applying these techniques to your KS3 revision will ensure you get better results in tests and assessments and will have all the relevant knowledge at your fingertips when you start studying for your GCSEs.

It really isn't rocket science either – you simply need to:

- **test yourself** on each topic as many times as possible
- **leave a gap** between the test sessions.

It is most effective if you leave a good period of time between the test sessions, e.g. between a week and a month. The idea is that just as you start to forget the information, you force yourself to recall it again, keeping it fresh in your mind.

Three Essential Revision Tips

1 **Use Your Time Wisely**
- Allow yourself plenty of time
- Try to start revising six months before tests and assessments – it's more effective and less stressful
- Your revision time is precious so use it wisely – using the techniques described on this page will ensure you revise effectively and efficiently and get the best results
- Don't waste time re-reading the same information over and over again – it's time-consuming and not effective!

2 **Make a Plan**
- Identify all the topics you need to revise (this Workbook will help you)
- Plan at least five sessions for each topic
- A one-hour session should be ample to test yourself on the key ideas for a topic
- Spread out the practice sessions for each topic – the optimum time to leave between each session is about one month but, if this isn't possible, just make the gaps as big as realistically possible.

3 **Test Yourself**
- Methods for testing yourself include: quizzes, practice questions, flashcards, past-papers, explaining a topic to someone else, etc.
- This Workbook gives you opportunities to check your progress
- Don't worry if you get an answer wrong – provided you check what the right answer is, you are more likely to get the same or similar questions right in future!

Visit our website to download your free flashcards, for more information about the benefits of these revision techniques and for further guidance on how to plan ahead and make them work for you.

www.collins.co.uk/collinsks3revision

Contents

Place Knowledge

Location Knowledge – Russia

Russia is the world's largest country. It stretches across both Europe and Asia and shares borders with more countries than any other.

1 Name the **three** Asian countries shown that share a land border with Russia.

_____ [3]

2 Which sea separates Russia from Iran? _____ [1]

3 Which Russian city offers a short sea route to the European capitals of Helsinki in Finland and Stockholm in Sweden? _____ [1]

4 The Russian city of Vladivostok is a port on which sea? _____ [1]

5 The city of Irkutsk is found on the shores of which huge lake? _____ [1]

6 Name **two** Russian rivers that discharge into the Arctic Ocean.

_____ [2]

7 Explain why Russia may find itself in conflict with neighbouring countries over fresh water supplies and the behaviour of some rivers.

_____

_____

_____ [4]

8 Name the countries on the map that along with Russia have an Arctic Ocean coastline.

....

....

....

....

.... [5]

9 Complete the paragraph using the words in the box below.

easier	Arctic	land	climate	frozen	trade

Russia has a large ocean coastline along the .... Ocean. Unlike Antarctica there

is no .... beneath this frozen wilderness. Throughout human history this ocean

has been ...., making transport impossible. This means that ....

routes for Russian produce have been much longer. However, due to ....

change, the sea ice has thinned making passage through the ice much .... [6]

10 Which sea separates Russia from the USA? .... [1]

11 If a person headed due **east** across the Arctic Ocean from the New Siberian Islands,

which country would they come across first? .... [1]

Total Marks .... / 26

Place Knowledge

Location Knowledge – China

Use the map below to answer the questions that follow.

1 Name **three** countries that share a land border with China.

.... [3]

2 Which sea separates China from South Korea? .... [1]

3 The island of Hainan Dao is found in what sea? .... [1]

4 The cities of Xiamen and Fuzhou face Taiwan over what body of water? .... [1]

5 Which city is found at the mouth of the Xi Jiang River? .... [1]

6 Which **two** rivers discharge into the Yellow Sea?

.... [2]

7 Explain why China's cities tend to be clustered around the East Coast and rivers.

....

.... [2]

Use the map below to answer the questions that follow.

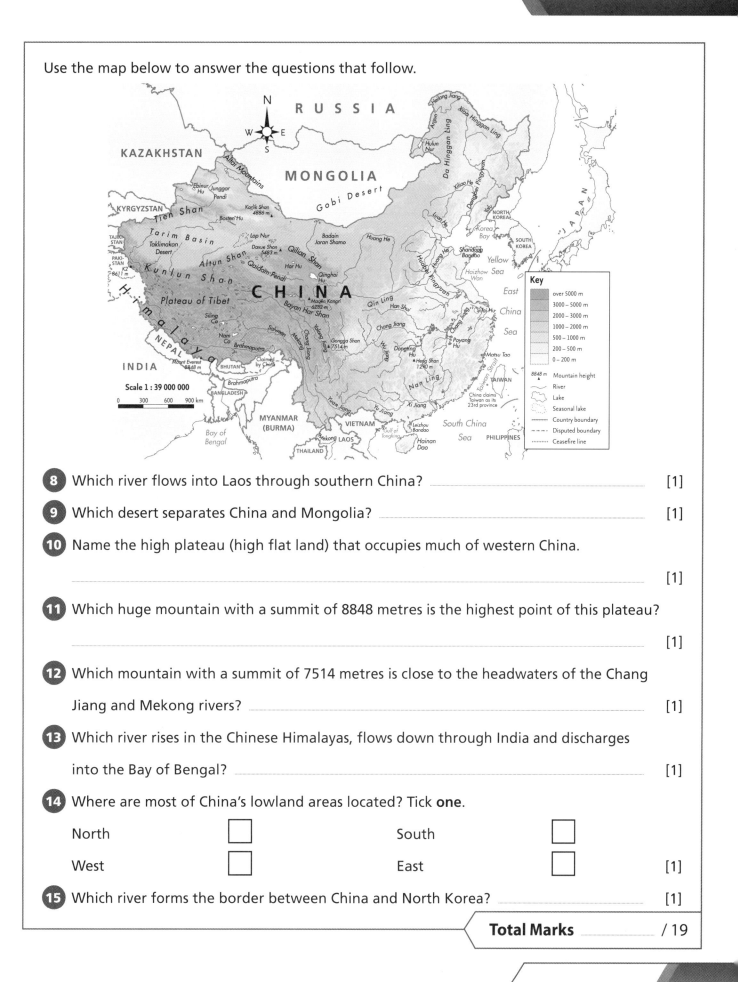

8 Which river flows into Laos through southern China? .... [1]

9 Which desert separates China and Mongolia? .... [1]

10 Name the high plateau (high flat land) that occupies much of western China.

.... [1]

11 Which huge mountain with a summit of 8848 metres is the highest point of this plateau?

.... [1]

12 Which mountain with a summit of 7514 metres is close to the headwaters of the Chang

Jiang and Mekong rivers? .... [1]

13 Which river rises in the Chinese Himalayas, flows down through India and discharges

into the Bay of Bengal? .... [1]

14 Where are most of China's lowland areas located? Tick **one**.

North ☐ South ☐

West ☐ East ☐ [1]

15 Which river forms the border between China and North Korea? .... [1]

Total Marks .... / 19

Place Knowledge

Use the map below to answer the questions that follow.

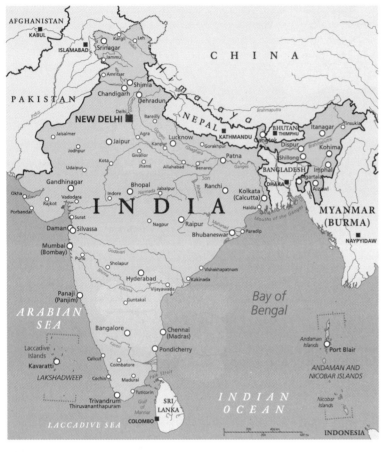

1. Name **three** countries that share a land border with India.

   _____

   _____

   _____ [3]

2. Which body of water separates India from Myanmar?

   _____ [1]

3. The Laccadive Islands are found in which sea?

   _____ [1]

4. Which river discharges into the Arabian Sea to the south of the city of Gandhinagar?

   _____ [1]

5. Which major city is found at the mouth of the Ganges River?

   _____ [1]

6. Name **two** rivers that discharge into the Bay of Bengal.

   _____ [2]

7. Many of India's rivers, e.g. Ganges, Brahmaputra, start in, or flow into other countries. Suggest some of the problems this might cause.

   _____

   _____

   _____

   _____ [4]

Use the map below to answer the questions that follow.

8 Name **three** mountains in India that are higher than 2000 metres.

_____ [3]

9 Which huge mountain range separates India from China? _____ [1]

10 Which desert separates India from Pakistan? _____ [1]

11 Name the high plateau (high flat land) that separates the Western and Eastern Ghats.

_____ [1]

12 Which mountain with a summit of 2695 metres is the highest point of this plateau?

_____ [1]

13 Which coastal mountain in the Eastern Ghats reaches a height of 1501 metres?

_____ [1]

14 The Arabian Sea is the most northern part of which ocean? _____ [1]

Total Marks _____ / 22

Place Knowledge

Location Knowledge – The Middle East

Use the map below to answer the questions that follow.

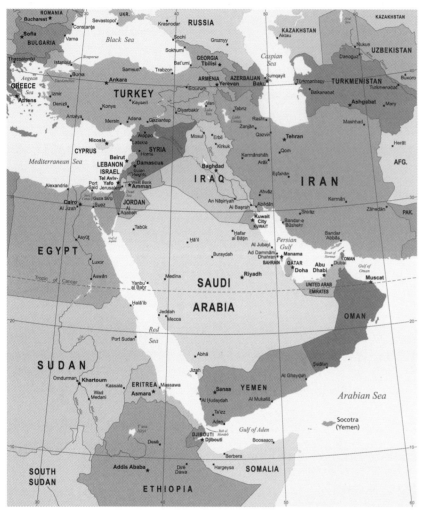

1 Name **three** countries that share a land border with Saudi Arabia.

....

....

.... [3]

2 Which sea separates Egypt and Turkey?

....

.... [1]

3 Name **three** countries that have a coastline on the Black Sea.

....

....

.... [3]

4 Cairo lies directly on what line of latitude? .... [1]

5 Which important and named line of latitude runs through Egypt, Saudi Arabia, The United Arab Emirates and Oman? .... [1]

6 To which country does the island of Socotra belong? .... [1]

7 Through which **three** countries does the Euphrates River flow?

.... [3]

Use the map below to answer questions 9–11.

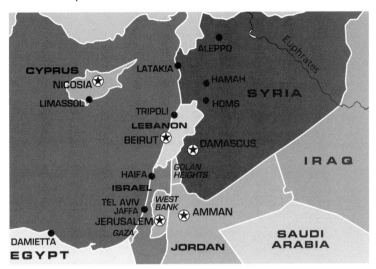

8 Fill in the gaps in the paragraph using the words in the box below.

| separate | Levant | conflict | Holocaust | Jewish | Muslim | Christian |

The countries and areas in the map above are commonly referred to as the ....

These countries and areas have been the sites of much .... throughout

the centuries. Jordan, Egypt, Syria, Iraq and Saudi Arabia are majority ....

countries. Israel, set up officially after the .... of the Second World War, is a

majority .... state. Lebanon and Cyprus both have sizeable ....

communities, which in Lebanon's case live happily alongside their Muslim countrymen but in

Cyprus they live in .... parts of the country. [7]

9 Name **two** areas seemingly located within the state of Israel that appear to have uncertain
borders.

....

[1]

10 Using your own knowledge, suggest which sea is found in the western part of the map
above.

....

[1]

11 Turkey, which borders Syria to the north, is building dams on the Euphrates River.
Suggest **two** issues for Syria that could arise because of this.

....

....

[2]

| **Total Marks** .... | / 24 |

Place Knowledge

Location Knowledge – Nigeria

Use the map below to answer the questions that follow.

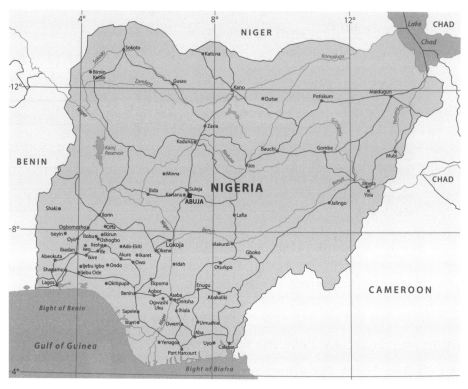

1. Name **three** countries that share a land border with Nigeria.

   _____ [3]

2. Port Harcourt is found at the delta of which river? _____ [1]

3. Name a city that can be found at the confluence of two rivers. _____ [1]

4. Which river crosses into Nigeria from northern Cameroon? _____ [1]

5. Name a lake that forms part of Nigeria's border. _____ [1]

6. Name a Nigerian city that lies on or is closest to the following lines of latitude (°N) or longitude (°E).

   a) 12°N _____

   b) 8°N _____

   c) 4°E _____

   d) 8°E _____ [4]

Use the map below to answer question 7.

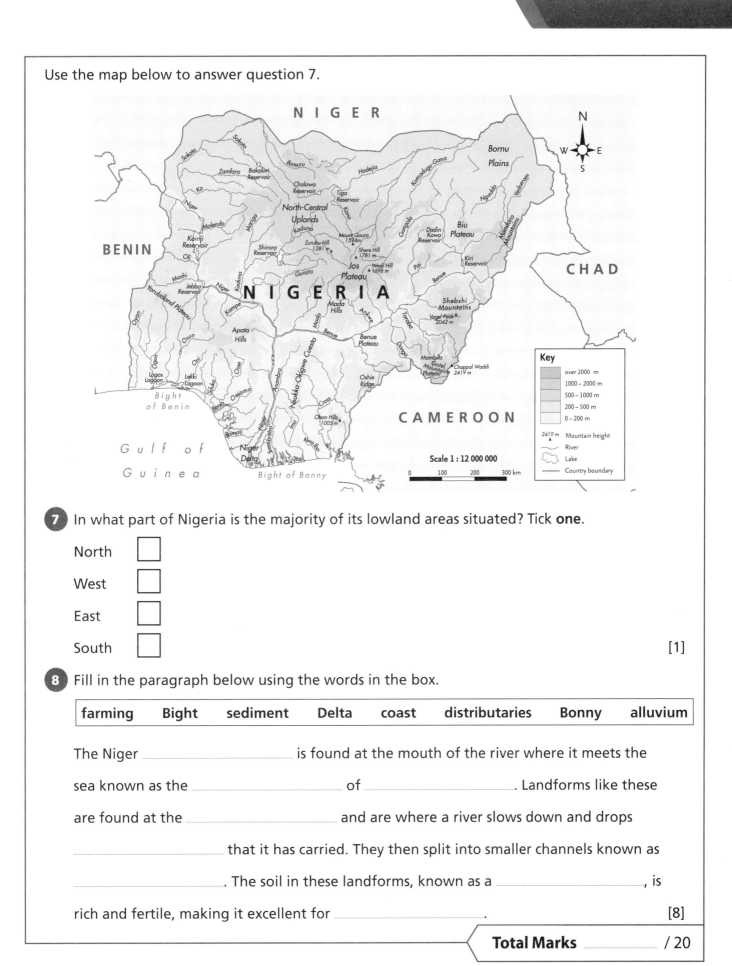

7　In what part of Nigeria is the majority of its lowland areas situated? Tick **one**.

North ☐

West ☐

East ☐

South ☐   [1]

8　Fill in the paragraph below using the words in the box.

farming	Bight	sediment	Delta	coast	distributaries	Bonny	alluvium

The Niger _____ is found at the mouth of the river where it meets the

sea known as the _____ of _____. Landforms like these

are found at the _____ and are where a river slows down and drops

_____ that it has carried. They then split into smaller channels known as

_____. The soil in these landforms, known as a _____, is

rich and fertile, making it excellent for _____.   [8]

Total Marks _____ / 20

Place Knowledge

Use the map below to answer the questions that follow.

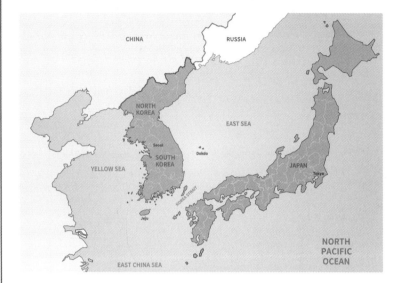

1 Name the **three** countries closest to South Korea.

....

....

.... [3]

2 Which sea separates South Korea and China?

.... [1]

Use the map below to answer the questions that follow.

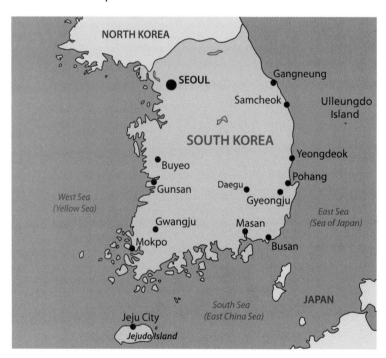

3 What is the capital city of South Korea? .... [1]

4 Name an island in the South Sea. .... [1]

5 What is the South Sea also known as? .... [1]

6 Name an island in the East Sea. .... [1]

7 What is the East Sea also known as? .... [1]

Use the map below to answer the questions that follow.

8 Which river flows into the Korea Strait near the city of Busan? _____ [1]

9 Which river flows into the Yellow Sea near the city of Gunsan? _____ [1]

10 Which **two** rivers join at a confluence to the east of the city of Seoul?

_____ [1]

11 How high in metres is Jiri-san mountain in southern South Korea? _____ [1]

12 How high is Seoraksan mountain in the north-east of South Korea? _____ [1]

13 Fill in the gaps in the paragraph using the words in the box below.

peninsula	south	mountainous	Asia	north	Taebaek	water

South Korea is a small country in eastern _____. It is a _____,

meaning it is bordered on three sides by _____. It is a _____

country with lowlands found in the _____. South Korea's biggest upland area,

known as the _____ mountains, are found in the far _____ east,

close to its border with North Korea. [7]

Total Marks _____ / 21

Progress Test 1

The map below shows China.

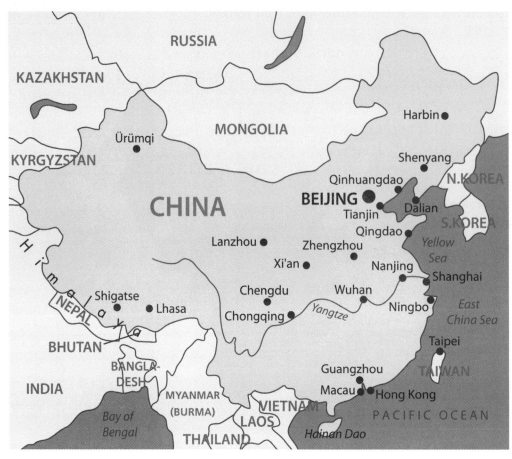

1. Name **one** country that shares a land border with China.

_____ [1]

2. By being on or near the coast, what advantages do Beijing and Shanghai have?

_____

_____ [2]

3. Give **three** problems for people who live in the Himalaya mountains region of south-eastern China.

_____

_____

_____ [3]

4. What are Hainan Dao and Taiwan that South and North Korea are not?

_____ [1]

5. Name a country that shares a land border with India.

_____ [1]

6 This photograph shows the sprawling metropolis of Seoul, the capital city of South Korea.

The list below shows **challenges** and **opportunities** of life in Seoul. Identify them by placing a **C** or **O** in the appropriate boxes.

Air pollution ☐

Job opportunities ☐

High land values ☐

Choice of lifestyle ☐

Social isolation ☐

Excellent transport links ☐

Close to hostile neighbouring country ☐

Traffic congestion ☐ [8]

7 Which of these natural disasters are caused by India's location at the head of the Bay of Bengal? Tick **two**.

Floods ☐   Earthquakes ☐

Tropical storms ☐   Tornadoes ☐ [2]

8 The photograph below shows the Dharavi slum in Mumbai.

Give **three** challenges the people of the Dharavi slum in Mumbai might face.

....

....   **[3]**

9 Turkey, Georgia and Russia all have coastlines on which sea?

....   **[1]**

10 Name **three** countries in the Middle East that the Tropic of Cancer runs through.

....   **[3]**

11 Name **one** country that shares a land border with Nigeria. ....   **[1]**

12 This is a photograph of the confluence of the Niger and Benue rivers in Nigeria.

What does the word confluence mean?

....   **[1]**

13 The Benue River starts in Cameroon, a country that borders Nigeria. State **two** problems this could cause.

....

....

.... [2]

14 What is meant by the term peninsula, for example the Arabian Peninsula?

.... [2]

15 Name the country that shares a land border with South Korea.

.... [1]

16 Name the nation of islands that lies across the East Sea from South Korea.

.... [1]

17 The map below shows the location of Russia on a world map.

Which **two** continents does Russia lie over?

.... [2]

18 What opportunities does the Arctic Ocean provide Russia?

.... [2]

19 In what part of Russia is Moscow, its capital city? Tick the correct answer.

North ☐   West ☐   East ☐   [1]

Total Marks .... / 38

Physical Geography

1 The different words used to describe different lengths of geological time are given below. Put them into the correct order by putting 1 in the box next to the longest through to 5 next to the shortest.

Period	
Age	
Eon	
Epoch	
Era	

[4]

2 a) Give **one** way that geologists try to work out the age of rocks.

.... [1]

b) Sometimes older rocks are found above younger rocks. Suggest **one** way that the rock layers may have had their original pattern changed.

....

.... [2]

3 The timeline below represents, to scale, the last 540 million years.

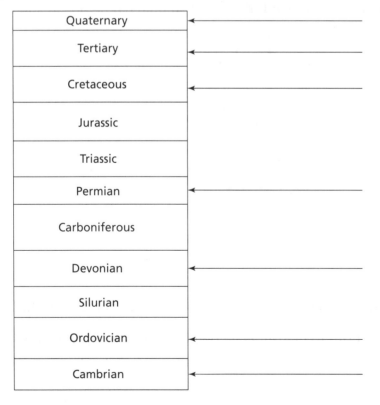

Quaternary ←
Tertiary ←
Cretaceous ←
Jurassic
Triassic
Permian ←
Carboniferous
Devonian ←
Silurian
Ordovician ←
Cambrian ←

a) Why are the divisions different sizes?

.... [1]

b) Seven of the divisions have an arrow alongside. Write 'humans' on the arrow next to the time when humans first appeared. [1]

c) Look at the pictures below.

 Trilobite   Reptile   Mammal

 Fish   Ammonite   Coral

Write the name of the life forms on the timeline arrows. [5]

4 Scientists have introduced the term 'Anthropocene' to the geological time scale. It is happening now, and is based on evidence that the atmosphere, water systems, sediments and vegetation are being changed by human activities rather than 'natural' forces. Some of the factors said to contribute to the Anthropocene are shown on the charts below.

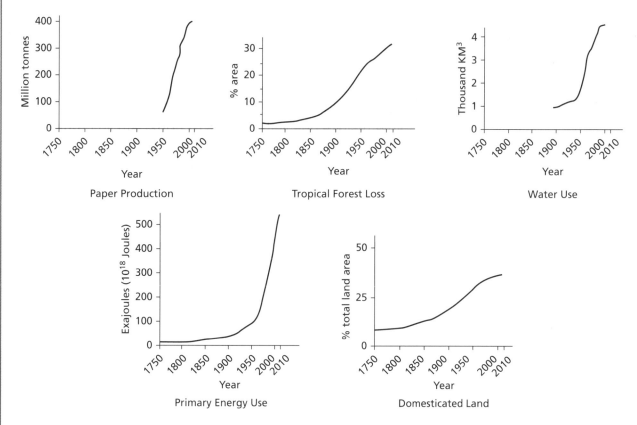

Paper Production

Tropical Forest Loss

Water Use

Primary Energy Use

Domesticated Land

Choose any **two** charts and explain how the changes shown contribute to the idea of the Anthropocene.

Factor 1 .... Explanation ....

....

....

....

[3]

Factor 2 .... Explanation ....

....

....

....

[3]

Total Marks .... / 20

Physical Geography

1 Draw lines to complete the sentences.

Tectonic plates move apart	is made of iron and nickel.
The Earth's core	at plate margins.
The mantle	at destructive margins.
Earthquakes occur most often	at ocean ridges.
Fold mountains form	is denser than the crust.

[4]

2 Look at the diagram below showing possible volcano locations.

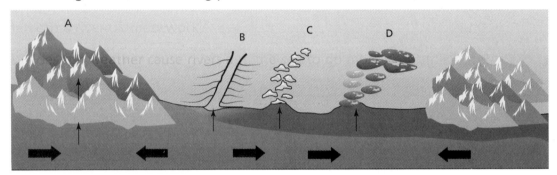

 Locations of volcanoes　　➡ Plate movement

Choose **one** of the locations A, B, C or D and explain why there are volcanoes present.

Location ....

Reason for volcanoes ....

....

....

[3]

3 The chart below gives some information about four volcanic eruptions.

Volcano name	Date of eruption	Number of deaths	V.E.I. (strength of eruption) max 8
Karakatau (also known as Krakatoa)	1883	37 000	6
Mount St Helens	1980	57	5
Nevado del Ruiz	1985	23 000	3
Pinatubo	1991	847	6

Stronger eruptions do not always cause more deaths and there have been eruptions with no associated deaths. Suggest some of the reasons for higher and lower numbers of deaths as a result of volcanic eruptions.

[6]

4 Complete the crossword using the clues below.

[12]

ACROSS

3 zone where plates dip (10)

7 magma at Earth's surface (4)

8 an instrument that measures earthquakes (11)

9 lava movement (4)

10 emitted from some volcanoes (3)

11 scale on which the magnitude of an earthquake is measured (7)

DOWN

1 all the Earth as one land mass (7)

2 sleeping volcano (7)

4 margin where plates slide past each other (12)

5 volcano with layers of different material (9)

6 emitted from some volcanoes (3)

12 number of major Earth structure layers (5)

Total Marks _____ / 25

Physical Geography

Rocks and Geology

1 The diagram below shows the rock cycle.

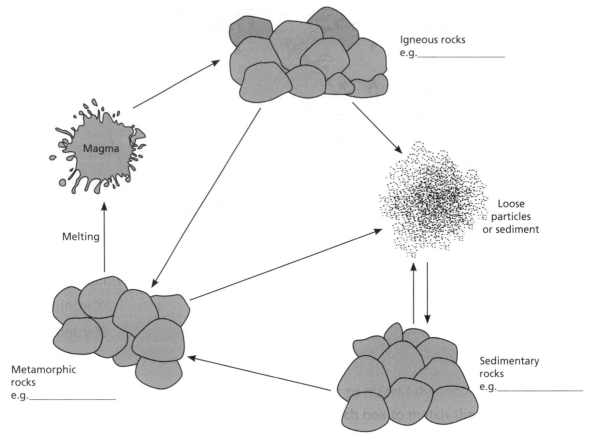

a) Give a named example of each rock type by filling in the gaps on the diagram. [3]

b) On the diagram, write what takes place in that part of the rock cycle along each arrow. One has been written in for you. [7]

2 **a)** Explain what a permeable rock is.

_____ [2]

b) The diagram below shows a porous rock, following days of heavy rainfall. In the space alongside it, draw a permeable rock after the same heavy rainfall.

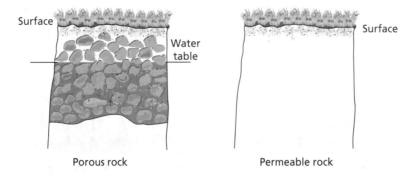

[2]

3 Most sedimentary rocks are formed under the sea or lakes. The picture below shows some layers that have formed under a lake.

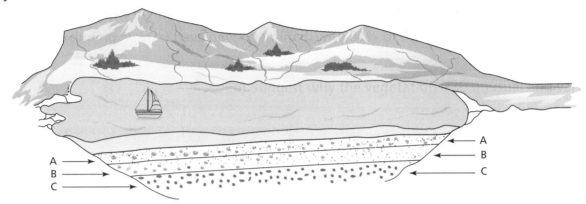

a) Which layer, A, B or C, is the oldest? .... [1]

b) Using the picture, identify the sources of the sediment and outline the ways in which it becomes layers under the lake.

....

....

....

....

[4]

4 The diagram below shows an area that has some igneous rocks in its landscape.

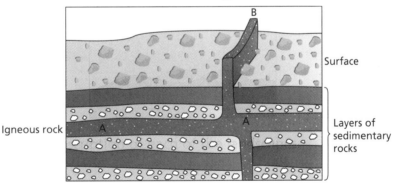

a) Explain how the features labelled A were formed.

....

....

[2]

b) Suggest why B is higher than the surrounding land.

....

[1]

Total Marks .... / 22

Physical Geography

Weathering and Soil

1 Look at the diagram below showing how effective mechanical weathering is in different climates.

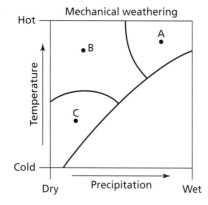

a) Which zone, A, B or C, has the **most** effective conditions for mechanical weathering?

.... [1]

b) Give **one** reason for your choice of answer to **a)**.

....

.... [2]

c) Which zone, A, B or C, has the **least** effective conditions for mechanical weathering? .... [1]

2 **a)** What is always required for chemical weathering to take place?

.... [1]

b) Look at the diagram below showing how effective chemical weathering is in different climates.

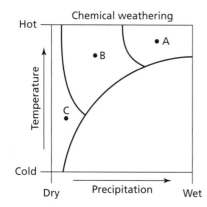

i) Which zone, A, B or C, has the **most** effective conditions for chemical weathering?

.... [1]

ii) Give **one** reason for your choice of answer to **i)**.

....

.... [2]

iii) Which zone, A, B or C, has the **least** effective conditions for chemical weathering?

.... [1]

3 The labelled field sketch below is of a mountaintop in the UK.

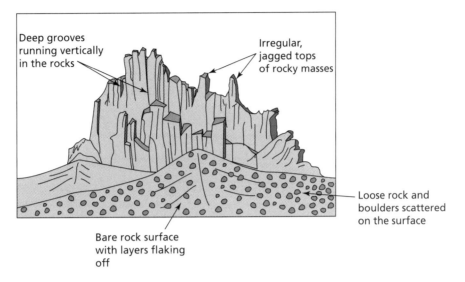

Deep grooves running vertically in the rocks

Irregular, jagged tops of rocky masses

Loose rock and boulders scattered on the surface

Bare rock surface with layers flaking off

Outline some of the weathering processes which, over time, could have contributed to the formation of this landscape.

....

....

....

....

.... [4]

4 Look at the diagram below of soil horizons.

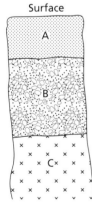

Surface

A

B

C

a) Describe the differences between horizons A and B.

....

....

....

.... [3]

b) What is horizon C made of? .... [1]

c) Describe **one** effect that horizon C can have on the soil formed above it.

....

.... [2]

Total Marks .... / 19

Progress Test 2

1 Rivers such as the Niger deposit alluvium in their lower course. Which group of people would find alluvium useful? _____ [1]

2 **a)** Number the following life forms in order of age, with the oldest first (1).

| Corals | Amphibians | Algae | Birds | Fish |

[4]

b) Sandstones can be formed from ocean deposits or from desert deposits. Put the letter 'O' for ocean or 'D' for desert next to the characteristics in the chart.

Characteristic	Ocean or desert?
Dark red	
Contains fossils	
Contains salt	
Found with limestones	

[3]

3 Suggest **two** benefits to Nigeria of Lake Chad on its north-eastern border with Chad.

_____ [2]

4 The dots on the map below show the location of earthquakes in early 2020. The bigger the dot, the stronger the earthquake.

a) Why did these earthquakes not get reported on national news?

_____ [1]

b) All of the earthquakes registered on the magnitude scale but only three registered on the intensity scale. What is the difference between magnitude and intensity of earthquakes?

_____

_____ [2]

c) What is the key difference in the scales of magnitude and intensity?

_____

_____ [2]

5 Why is it unwise to plough a field when the soil is very wet?

_____

_____ [3]

6 Suggest **one** benefit of South Korea's position as a peninsula.

_____ [1]

7 The main areas of rock from six geological periods are shown on the maps below.
Match each map to the period in the chart.

A  B  C

D  E  F

Map letter	Geological time period
	Cretaceous
	Jurassic
	Triassic
	Carboniferous
	Devonian
	Cambrian

[5]

8 Match up the type of rock with its use.

Granite	Ground in cement
Sandstone	Gravestones; kitchen worktops
Marble	To make 'stone-wash' denim for jeans
Limestone	Roofs
Basalt	Building material
Slate	Decorative sculpture
Pumice	Crushed for use in concrete

[6]

9 Most of the largest cities in the west of China are on flat land; why is this?

_____

_____ [2]

10 Sapphire, ruby, aquamarine and beryl are all precious gemstones which can be found in north-west Scotland and the Western Islands. There are no precious gemstones in south-east England.

a) What does this tell us about gemstones?

_____ [1]

b) In what type of rock do gemstones seem to be found? _____ [1]

11 The diagrams below are of three volcano shapes.

a) Which emits the runniest, least viscous lava? _____ [1]

b) Which emits the thickest, most viscous lava? _____ [1]

c) State **three** other materials that can be ejected from volcanoes.

_____ [3]

12 After which global conflict was the country of Israel set up?

_____ [1]

13 All sedimentary rocks break down into smaller pieces. Put the list of particle descriptions below into size order, with the largest as number 1.

Gravel	
Cobble	
Sand	
Boulder	

[3]

14 Name **one** Asian country that shares a land border with Russia. _____ [1]

15 a) What is meant by 'seismic hazard'? _____ [1]

b) What are some of the forms that seismic hazards can take? Name **two**.

_____ [2]

16 Which Indian city is found at the mouth of the Ganges River? Tick the correct city.

Calcutta ☐   Mumbai ☐

Delhi ☐   Chennai ☐   [1]

17 a) A school has some samples of a rock called gneiss. This rock was formed at least 2600 million years ago. Which part of the UK is it likely to have come from?

_____ [1]

b) Slate is very hard and is made from clays which are very soft. What happened to the clays to form slate?

_____ [2]

c) On a beach there are pebbles of sandstone with white 'stripes' that stick out. Why do the white stripes stick out?

_____ [1]

d) What are the white stripes in the pebble described in **c)** likely to be made of?

_____ [1]

18 Following the end of the Second World War, countries such as South Korea achieved rapid economic development – they were said to have roared ahead. Countries like South Korea were given a nickname. What is this nickname? Choose from the list.

Supernations ☐   Jumping Beans ☐

Asian Tigers ☐   Go-getters ☐   [1]

19 What is meant by 'soil erosion'? _____ [1]

20 The following are **challenges** and **opportunities** of living in the Thar Desert of north-west India. Identify them by placing a **C** or **O** in the appropriate boxes.

Tourism ☐   Mineral deposits ☐

Long growing season ☐   Little access to clean water ☐

Very high temperatures ☐   Conflict with neighbouring country ☐

Little will grow ☐   Little transport infrastructure ☐   [8]

Total Marks _____ / 63

Physical Geography

1 The two maps below show the isotherms for January and July in Great Britain. An isotherm is a line that joins up places of the same temperature.

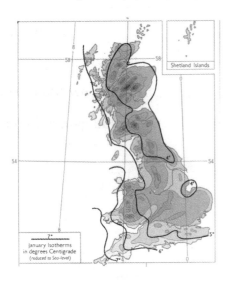 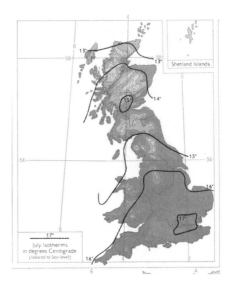

Complete the passage below using the words in the box.

warmer	north	south	land	lowest
south-east	west	cooler	north-west	

In January, the isotherms generally run from _____ to south. The sea tends to be _____ than the land. Temperatures in _____ Scotland are similar to those in south-east England. The _____ temperatures are along the North Sea coast.

In July, temperatures increase towards the _____. Isotherms run from _____ to east and bend north over _____ showing that the sea is _____ than the land. The highest temperatures are in the _____ of England.

[9]

2 The map below shows Great Britain split into regions A, B, C and D.

a) Using the information on the isotherm maps in **Q1** and the map above, put the correct letters, A, B, C or D into the table.

Description	Mild winters, warm summers	Mild winters, cool summers	Cold winters, cool summers	Cold winters, warm summers
Region (letter)				

[3]

b) Identify **one** influence on temperature and explain how it causes temperatures to be higher or lower than might be expected. ....

....

.... [3]

3 The map below shows mean annual precipitation in Great Britain.

Gt. Britain Precipitation

☐ <625 mm

▨ 625–750 mm

▤ 751–1000 mm

▦ 1001–1500 mm

◼ >1500 mm

a) What is the lowest total precipitation in Great Britain? .... [1]

b) Which parts of Great Britain are driest?

.... [1]

c) One of the areas experiencing the highest precipitation totals is north-west Scotland. Suggest **one** reason for this.

....

....

.... [2]

Physical Geography

4 The charts below are for a town in Great Britain. It is one of those labelled P, Q, R or S on the map below.

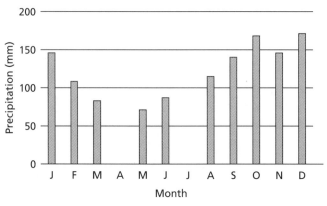

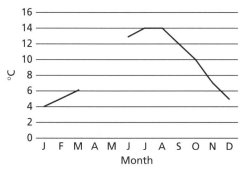

	April	May	July
mm	90		120
°C	7	11	

a) Complete the charts using the figures given in the table above. [4]

b) The total precipitation for the town is 1451 mm. The monthly average (mean) precipitation is 120 mm. How many months are wetter than average? .... [1]

c) Give **one** reason why the monthly average (mean) precipitation amount is not a very useful piece of information.

....

.... [2]

d) To which town, P, Q, R or S do the figures and charts refer? .... [1]

5 The chart below shows the top ten hottest and coolest years on record.

Hottest years	2014	2006	2011	2007	2017	2003	2018	2004	2002	2005
Coolest years	1892	1888	1885	1963	1919	1886	1917	1909	1887	1962

Compare the two sets of dates.

....

....

....
[3]

6 **a)** Since 1900 temperatures on planet Earth have been gradually getting warmer. One of the changes to the climate system resulting from this warming is that ice is melting. Ice in the Arctic is 65% thinner now than it was in 1975. Discuss some of the other changes to the climate system that result from rising temperatures.

....

....

....

....

....
[6]

b) Changes to the climate system have had many impacts on the natural and human world. To help pupils understand what is happening, a primary school is making a set of single-sentence information boards to put around a green space in their grounds. One is shown below.

AS TEMPERATURES RISE

PLANTS BUD AND FLOWER EARLIER

Choose any **other** impact and create a design in the space below. Use any style of lettering and colouring that you wish.

[3]

Total Marks .... / 39

Physical Geography

Glaciation

1 Look at the diagram of an area that was glaciated in the past.

a) Draw a line from side to side across the diagram to show how high ice is likely to have reached. [1]

b) Explain why you have chosen that position.

....

.... [2]

2 Corrie lakes (sometimes called tarns) and ribbon lakes are two kinds of lake found in glaciated areas such as the Lake District in England. Give **one** difference between the two types of lake.

....

.... [2]

3 Look at the sketch map below which shows part of the Lake District.

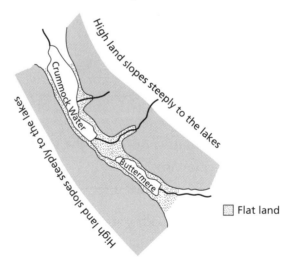

Buttermere and Crummock Water were a single lake when the ice retreated from this area.

Explain why there are now two lakes instead of just one.

....

.... [3]

4 Over a very long time, as glaciers move across land, they can erode it. This is glacial erosion. What do you understand by the term 'glacial erosion'?

....

.... [2]

5 Give **two** differences between the shape of a river valley and a glaciated valley.

.... [2]

6 Give an example of a leisure activity that people can take part in as a result of the changes caused by glaciation to a river valley and explain why.

....

.... [2]

7 There are no longer glaciers in the British Isles. Explain **two** differences, compared to our present climate, that enabled glaciers to form in the past.

Difference 1 ....

....

Difference 2 ....

.... [4]

8 The sentence below is taken from *The Times* newspaper of 6 January 2020. It is part of a report about an application to allow houseboats on Grasmere, a small lake in the Lake District.

Locals say the unspoilt Lake District landscape will soon be 'desecrated' if the landowner gets permission from the National Park to put ten motor yachts on the lake for holidaymakers.

a) Why might some people say that the landscape is not 'unspoilt'?

....

.... [2]

b) Why might some groups of people be concerned if permission for the houseboats is granted?

....

....

.... [3]

Total Marks .... / 23

Physical Geography

Rivers and Coasts

1 Moving water in rivers and the sea can erode and carry material, causing the landscape to change. This requires energy.

a) From where does the water in rivers get its energy? .... [1]

b) Where in the sea is the energy that can be used for erosion and transport?

.... [1]

c) For most of the time, rivers in the UK do almost no erosion or transport. What is the river's energy used for?

.... [1]

d) When can a river do most work? .... [1]

e) How does the weather cause rivers and the sea to do more erosion and transportation?

....

....

....

.... [4]

2 Look at the sketch of the course of a river shown below. The river is flowing from west to east.

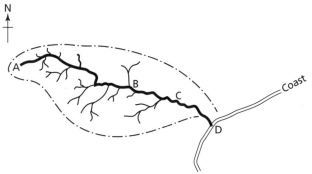

a) Complete the table by putting the correct letters next to the feature.

Feature	Letter
Meander	
Source	
Mouth	
Confluence	

[4]

b) What is represented by the dot-and-dash line on the diagram? .... [1]

A stream or river which flows into another is a tributary. The river in the diagram has many more tributaries reaching the river from the south than the north.

c) Give **one** factor to explain why there might be such a difference in the number of tributaries.

.... [2]

d) This river flows straight into the sea. Complete the sentence below to state **two** other ways in which a river reaches the sea and then describe them.

A river can reach the sea as .... or ....

Descriptions ....

....

.... [4]

3 Orfordness Lighthouse in Suffolk was built in 1792, several hundred metres from the sea. In 2005, it was 20 metres from the sea, in 2015 it was 10 metres from the sea, and in January 2020, when the photo below was taken, the lighthouse had to be closed.

Location of Orfordness lighthouse

a) What does the information about Orfordness Lighthouse suggest about coastal erosion?

....

.... [2]

b) Describe **one** way in which the sea might be causing the area around the lighthouse to collapse.

....

.... [2]

c) In 2016, huge sacks of gravel and shingle were placed around the base of the lighthouse as protection. Some groups and individuals did not want this to happen. Discuss why there are different opinions about coastal protection.

....

....

....

....

....

.... [6]

Total Marks .... / 29

Physical Geography

1 Study the world map below.

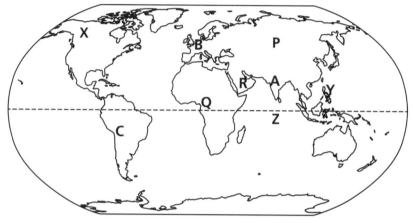

a) Draw the Tropic of Cancer and the Arctic Circle on the map. [2]

b) Name the following:

i) Country X: ....

ii) Country Y: ....

iii) Ocean Z: .... [3]

2 a) The climate information in the boxes below refers to places labelled A, B or C on the world map. Circle **one** of the letters A, B or C in **each** box to match the information with the location on the map.

Lowest temperature: January 5°C Highest temperature: August 20°C Total precipitation: 900 mm A B C	Lowest temperature: July 14°C Highest temperature: January 20°C Total precipitation: 2.3 mm A B C	Lowest temperature: December 20°C Highest temperature: April, May and June 30°C Total precipitation: 1601 mm A B C

[3]

b) Look at the sketches of natural vegetation shown below. Each belongs to **one** of the areas labelled P, Q or R on the world map. Circle **one** of the letters P, Q or R under **each** sketch to match the vegetation with the location on the map.

 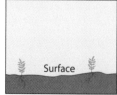 

P   Q   R   P   Q   R   P   Q   R   [3]

3 The shaded area on the map of Australia shows a region where there has been no ice for 200 million years. There has been no geological disturbance for tens of millions of years. The soils are very low in nutrients. There is an exceptionally varied vegetation. 7239 plant varieties (excluding mosses) have been identified, with 80% of these not found anywhere else.

a) Suggest why the vegetation is so unusual and varied.

....

....

....

....

[4]

b) As in many other areas of the world, the vegetation of South-West Australia is under threat. What might be causing problems for the vegetation?

....

....

....

....

[4]

4 The pictures below represent different types of landscape.

i)   **ii)**   **iii)**

a) Write a short, simple description of each of the landscapes.

i) ....

ii) ....

iii) .... [3]

b) For **any** of the landscapes, suggest challenges to humans living there.

....

....

[2]

Total Marks .... / 24

Progress Test 3

1 Which country to the north-east of India is almost completely surrounded by India on its western, eastern and northern sides? Choose from the list below.

Bangladesh ☐   Pakistan ☐

Thailand ☐   Sri Lanka ☐   [1]

2 Fossils are preserved remains of plants and animals.

a) In what type of environment were they formed?

.... [2]

b) State **two** parts of an animal that would be preserved as a fossil.

.... [2]

c) How do fossils help with reconstruction of the history of the Earth?

....

.... [3]

3 Which country does the Mekong River flow south from China into? Choose **one** from the list.

Laos ☐   India ☐

Bangladesh ☐   Russia ☐   [1]

4 Which Egyptian city lies directly on the 30° North line of latitude? Choose from the list below.

Alexandria ☐   Memphis ☐

Port Said ☐   Cairo ☐   [1]

5 **a)** Rock surfaces in glaciated regions sometimes have smooth, polished surfaces and sometimes have rugged surfaces. How does moving ice produce these two different results?

....

....

.... [4]

b) What are the surface scratches caused by moving ice that are found on rocks called?

.... [1]

6 In the Niger Delta there is a large oil-drilling industry. Unfortunately it has many problems. Tick **two** of its problems from the list below.

Threats from terrorists ☐   Low-quality oil ☐

Poor-quality pipeline infrastructure ☐   Other countries do not want to buy the oil ☐   [2]

7 **a)** In February 2020, some places in Britain experienced 'a month's rainfall in one day'. What does that mean?

_____

_____ [2]

b) What is meant by 'a 100-year flood event'?

_____

_____ [2]

8 The map below shows the location of Lake Baikal, which is close to Russia's border with Mongolia.

The following are **challenges** and **opportunities** of the lake. Identify them by placing a **C** or **O** in the appropriate boxes.

Tourism	☐	Remote location	☐
Access to fresh water	☐	Fishing industry	☐
Pollution by industry	☐	Overfishing	☐
High biodiversity	☐		[7]

9 Into which sea does the Huang He river discharge? Choose **one** sea from the list below.

Aral Sea	☐	Caspian Sea	☐
Mediterranean Sea	☐	Yellow Sea	☐ [1]

10 The table shows earthquakes that happened in late 2019–early 2020.

Date	Depth (km)	Magnitude	Intensity	Region
February 2020	10	3.2	4	North-west France
February 2020	142	7	6	Kuril Islands
January 2020	10	7.7	7	Caribbean Sea
January 2020	10	6.7	8	Eastern Turkey
December 2019	10	6.5	7	Puerto Rico
November 2019	18	6.8	7	Philippines
November 2019	22	6.4	8	Albania
October 2019	20	5.9	7	North-west Iran
October 2019	10	6.5	8	Philippines

a) In what way is north-west France a different type of location from the others in the list?

.... [1]

b) Why is the depth of the earthquake an important piece of information?

....

.... [2]

c) From the information given on the chart, assess which event would be considered the 'worst'.

....

....

.... [3]

11 Which of the following transnational corporations is South Korean in origin? Tick **one**.

Sony ☐ Huawei ☐

Apple ☐ Samsung ☐ [1]

12 Plants become adapted to their climate. For example, some plants have pale- or silver-coloured leaves to reflect very bright sunshine, which could cause water to be lost quickly so that the leaves would shrivel and the plant could suffer from lack of water. Describe a different plant adaptation and explain why it has developed.

Adaptation ....

Explanation ....

....

....

.... [4]

13 **a)** Coal from South Wales can contain fossils of ferns. What do they tell us about the formation of coal?

....

.... [2]

b) The pictures below are of ammonite fossils. Ammonites are extinct sea creatures but these fossils were found in mountains.

How can fossilised sea creature remains be found in mountains?

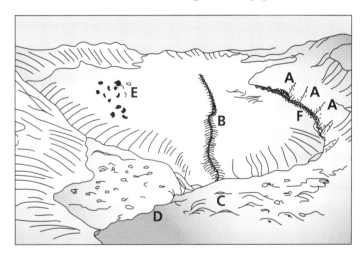

....

....

....

....

.... [3]

c) Within an area of sedimentary rock, where are the best fossils found?

.... [1]

14 **a)** The sketch below shows the front of a wasting/melting glacier.

Complete the table by adding the names of the features next to the letters as shown on the sketch.

A		D	
B		E	
C		F	

[6]

b) What is the front of a glacier called? .... [1]

15 After the Second World War, South Korea's rapid development was based on it having huge natural reserves of crude oil. Is this statement true or false? _____ [1]

16 The diagram below shows a waterfall. It has formed in an area of uniform rock type.

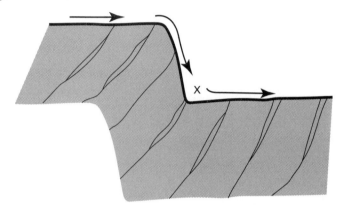

    a) What is the most likely cause of the waterfall? _____ [1]

    b) What feature could form at point X?

    _____ [1]

17 What is the difference between rain and drizzle?

_____ [1]

18 Some glaciated valleys have waterfalls at the sides. Explain how these waterfalls were formed.

_____

_____

_____

_____ [4]

19 Sedimentary rocks such as limestones have bedding planes and some have joints. What effect do bedding planes and joints have on the weathering of the rock?

_____

_____ [2]

20 The three landscapes drawn below all have a mean altitude of 250 metres.

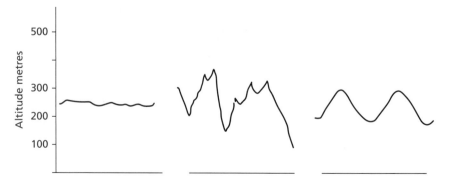

  a) Why is the mean altitude not always the most useful piece of information?

_____ [1]

b) What other information could be included to give a better idea of the landscapes?

_____ [1]

21 Here is a photograph of Nairobi, which is the largest city in Kenya.

From the reasons below, identify **four** pull factors that attract migrants to the city. Tick the correct boxes.

More jobs	☐	Education and healthcare	☐
Good cuisine	☐	Perception of the bright lights	
Jobs for unskilled workers	☐	of the big city	☐
High-quality housing for all	☐	Nice parks	☐ [4]

22 **a)** Complete the diagram below to show the action of longshore drift. [2]

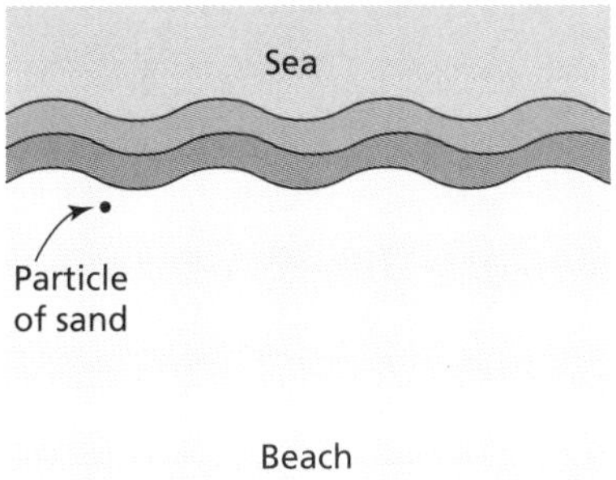

Sea

Particle
of sand

Beach

b) Explain why some holiday resorts try to prevent longshore drift.

_____

_____ [2]

23 **a)** Name the scale that is used to indicate the effects of wind that can be observed on land and sea. _____ [1]

b) What is meant by the term 'prevailing wind'?

_____ [1]

24 A beach is a feature of deposition of material by the sea. Name any **two** other deposition features. _____ [2]

25 Due to its huge expanse east–west, Russia has eleven of something. Tick **one** from the list below:

Seas	☐	Trade borders	☐
Time zones	☐	International agreements	☐ [1]

Total Marks _____ / 78

Human Geography

Population

1 Complete the paragraph using the words in the box below.

dense	sparse	distribution

Population _____ is the study of where people live. When people live

close together we call this _____ population. When people live more

spaced out we call this _____ population.   [3]

2 Study the map below.

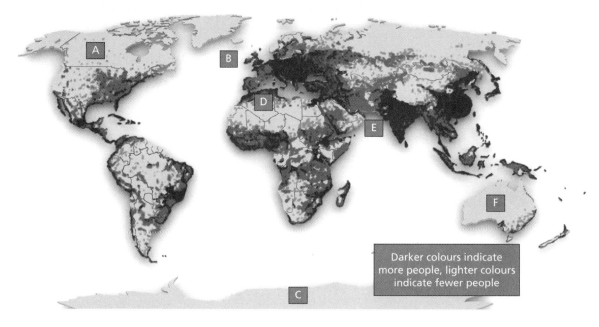

Darker colours indicate more people, lighter colours indicate fewer people

Use the map to say whether the places labelled have a dense or sparse population.
Circle the correct answer.

A Northern Canada   dense / sparse   **D** Sahara Desert   dense / sparse

B Western Europe   dense / sparse   **E** India   dense / sparse

C Antarctica   dense / sparse   **F** Central Australia   dense / sparse   [6]

3 Parts of the world are densely populated, and others are sparsely populated. Explain why
you think some parts of the world have dense populations and other less so.

_____

_____

_____

_____

_____   [6]

4 This diagram is called the J curve, for obvious reasons. It shows how the world's population has changed over the course of human history.

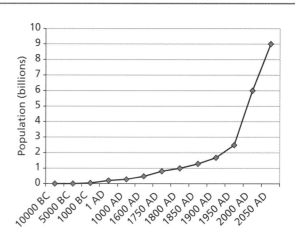

a) Which of the following are reasons why the world's population did not grow rapidly until around AD 1800? Tick **three**.

Lack of medicines ☐   Slow internet speeds ☐

Poor understanding of infectious disease ☐   Low amount of crops able to be grown ☐   [3]

Poor transport networks ☐

b) The world's population doubled in size between about AD 1700 and 1825. How many years did it take to double in size again? Tick **one**.

80 years ☐   100 years ☐   125 years ☐   [1]

5 This graph shows the UK's fertility rate (the average number of babies each woman has) between 1940 and 2010.

Use the graph to help fill in the gaps below. Circle the correct words to complete the sentences.

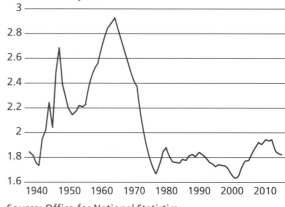

Total fertility rate, 1938–2015 (England and Wales)

Source: Office for National Statistics

After World War 2 in 1945, the UK's fertility rate peaked at .... babies per woman. In the mid-1960s it peaked again at about .... babies. The availability of contraceptives in the 1970s led to a big **drop/growth** in births. The rate is now between 1.7 and 1.8 because of **correlation/migration** from eastern Europe.   [4]

Total Marks .... / 23

Urbanisation

1 What is urbanisation? Tick **one** box.

The growth of towns and cities ☐   Reasons why people move to a city ☐

Movement of people away from cities ☐   A group of people who live in a city ☐   [1]

The graph below shows world urbanisation from 1950 to 2050.

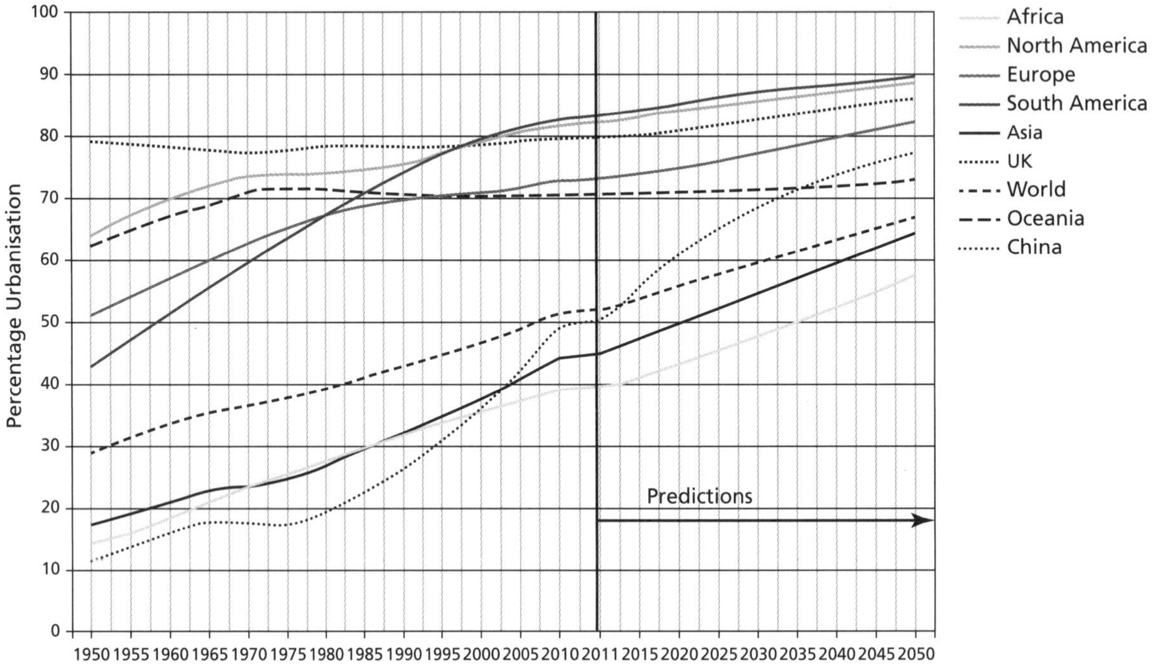

Use the graph to answer the following questions.

2 Which part of the world is predicted to have the highest level of urbanisation by 2050?

_____ [1]

3 Which part of the world experienced little growth in urbanisation from around 1970 onwards? _____ [1]

4 Which part of the world has experienced and is projected to continue experiencing the fastest urban growth between 1950 and 2050? _____ [1]

5 In 2011, when this graph was drawn, what percentage of the UK's population was urbanised?

_____ [1]

6 Suggest reasons why a country's level of urbanisation may begin to slow.

_____ [2]

Total Marks _____ / 7

Urbanisation: Case study – Rio de Janeiro, Brazil

This photograph is of a *favela* or squatter settlement in Rio de Janeiro.

1 Fill in the gaps in the paragraph using the words in the box below.

education	infrastructure	high	unplanned	crime

The *favela* lacks basic _____ like paved roads, sewers and electricity lines.

The *favela* is _____, therefore there is no control over how it has grown

and developed. Population density is very _____ as people live very close

together. Trust in the local police is low meaning that _____ is difficult

to control. The inhabitants of *favelas* are generally poor and have low access to good

_____ and healthcare. [5]

2 The government of the city of Rio de Janeiro started a project to improve these areas, known as the *slum-to-neighbourhood* (*favela–bairro* in Portuguese). Explain how the following things that the government did as part of the project could make life better for the inhabitants of *favelas*.

a) Ownership of the land on which their homes are built.

_____ [2]

b) Self-help schemes (giving people building materials).

_____ [2]

c) Cable cars from the top of the *favela* to the city centre.

_____ [2]

Total Marks _____ / 11

Human Geography

Development

The image below is of the Brandt Line, named after a German politician who was given the job in the late 1970s of separating the world into developed and developing nations. Today as geographers we try to use the terms **High Income Countries (HICs)**, **Low Income Countries (LICs)** and **Newly Emerging Economies (NEEs)**.

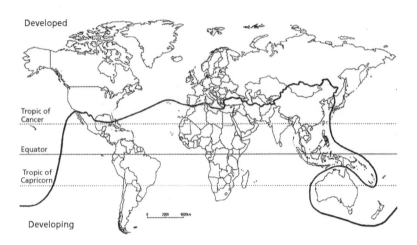

1. Use the map to help fill in the gaps.

    Countries to the n _____ of the line are said to be **developed** – they

    have a generally h _____ quality of life. Countries to the

    s _____ of the line are said to be **developing** – they have a generally

    l _____ quality of life. [4]

2. According to the map and using your own knowledge, classify the following countries as either developed or developing. Circle the correct answer.

    a) USA   developed / developing   **c)** India   developed / developing

    b) Brazil   developed / developing   **d)** UK   developed / developing   [4]

3. Outline what the following indicators of a country's development tell us about its quality of life. The first one has been done for you.

    a) Life expectancy – *a higher life expectancy suggests better healthcare in a country.*

    b) High birth rates – _____

    c) High literacy rates – _____

    d) Low unemployment – _____

    e) Few older people – _____   [4]

Total Marks _____ / 12

Development: Case study – China

The map below shows the location of China.

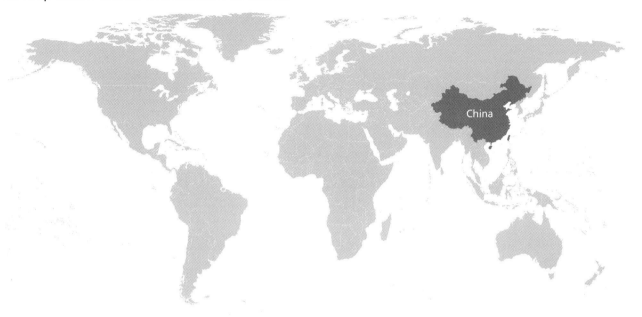

China

1 Use the words below to fill in the gaps in the text.

miracle	rural	Bank	foreign	labour	second	poverty	million

China today is the world's _____ largest economy but forty years ago it was

a poor, largely _____ nation with at least 30% of its population living in

_____. In 1980 China became a member of the World _____. As the

economy opened up to the outside world _____ companies flooded into China

to build factories and to take advantage of the cheap _____ (workers). More

than 500 _____ people have been lifted out of poverty since the reforms began.

It's been called an economic _____ .   [8]

2 Match up the beginning and end of each sentence.

Foreign companies like Apple use Chinese factories because...	... things from China as it is to make things in HICs like the UK.
Low shipping costs mean that it is just as cheap to ship...	... fewer rights in the workplace than British workers.
One reason for cheaper workers in China is that they have...	...lower wages mean higher profits.

[3]

Total Marks _____ / 11

Human Geography

Economic Activity

1 Place the jobs in the box into the Venn diagram.

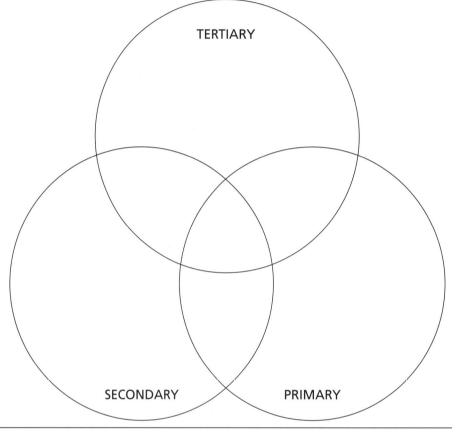

| coal miner | doctor | artist | farmer | postal worker |
| factory worker | builder | chef | lorry driver | police officer |

[10]

2 The following graph shows the percentage of employment in different sectors.

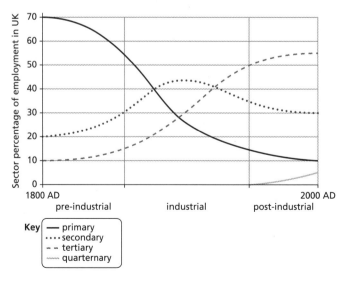

Use the graph to help fill in the gaps. Use the words below.

technology	primary	farming	secondary	tertiary
quaternary	mining	fishing	ship	

In the pre-industrial period, most people in the UK worked in _____

industry, in jobs like _____, _____ and

_____. During the industrial period, many more people became employed

in _____ industries in jobs such as steelmaking and _____

building. In the UK today, more people work in _____ industry selling

their time and skills. Jobs in today's _____ industries are often in research

and _____. [9]

3 Fill in the cumulative percentage bar charts below showing how the UK's employment in
the three sectors of industry has changed since the Industrial Revolution. The bar for 1801
has been done for you.

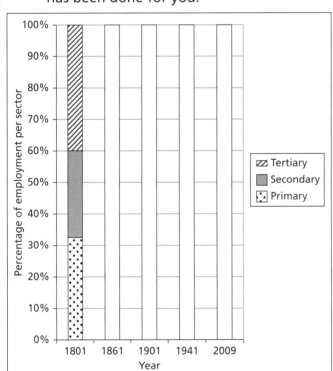

	Primary	Secondary	Tertiary
1801	33	27	40
1861	20	50	30
1901	10	60	30
1941	5	55	40
2009	3	37	60

[12]

4 Using knowledge you have already gained suggest **one** reason why fewer and fewer
people work in primary and secondary sector jobs in the UK today.

_____

_____ [1]

Total Marks _____ / 32

Human Geography

Natural Resources

The three natural resources critical to humans are water, food and energy. Resources can be **renewable** – they are naturally replenished – or **non-renewable** – once they are used up they are gone.

1 Arrange the **twelve** named resources below into the correct part of the page.

fish	coal	oil	wood	diamonds	wheat	cattle
limestone	natural gas	wind energy	solar energy	wave energy		

RENEWABLE | NON-RENEWABLE

[12]

2 The map below shows how much energy per capita (Latin for 'per person') each of the world's countries uses. It is measured in kilograms of oil equivalent.

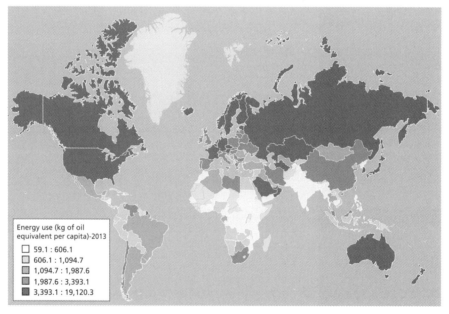

Energy use (kg of oil equivalent per capita)-2013
- 59.1 : 606.1
- 606.1 : 1,094.7
- 1,094.7 : 1,987.6
- 1,987.6 : 3,393.1
- 3,393.1 : 19,120.3

Name **three** countries that use energy within the highest usage bracket.

_____   _____   _____   [3]

3 Thinking about what you already know about economics, above which line do the majority of the high-energy-using countries sit? _____ [1]

4 Suggest reasons why some countries use a lot of energy.

_____ [2]

5 Of the six of the world's seven continents shown on the map, which of them uses overall the least energy per capita? _____ [1]

6 Suggest reasons why some countries use less energy than others.

_____ [2]

7 Here is a photo of a coal-fired power station in China.

Underline the statements that are **benefits** of the station in one colour. Underline the statements that are **drawbacks** in another colour.

Cheap power   Can lead to asthma in humans

Creates many jobs   Generates money for the country   [5]

Releases harmful gases

8 Here is a picture of a wind farm in Scotland.

Underline the statements that are **benefits** of the wind farm in one colour. Underline the statements that are **drawbacks** in another colour.

Some feel it ruins the landscape   Can affect migratory birds

Creates some jobs   Generates money for the local economy [5]

Releases no harmful gases

Total Marks _____ / 31

Progress Test 4

1 Complete the table below by stating whether each country is an HIC, LIC or NEE.

Brazil	UK	France	Afghanistan
....	....	....	....

[4]

2 Which geographical term describes the growth of towns and cities? Tick **one**.

Conurbation ☐

Counter-urbanisation ☐

Urbanisation ☐

Migration ☐

[1]

3 Choose and underline the correct % in each statement below when applied to the pre-Cambrian eon.

For 75% / 85% of the pre-Cambrian, the only life was single-celled.

The pre-Cambrian lasted for 66% / 88% of all geological time.

[2]

4 Which mountain range separates India and China? Tick **one**.

Andes ☐

Himalayas ☐

Atlas ☐

Zagros ☐

[1]

5 State the key characteristics of the landscape types shown in the table. The first one has been done for you.

Landscape type	Key characteristics
Urban	Dominated by buildings and man-made structures
Remote	
Rural	
Wetland	
Moorland	

[8]

6 Under each of the pictures below indicate whether they are a **renewable** or **non-renewable** energy source.

a)

b)

c)

d)

[4]

7 The land in glaciated areas such as the Lake District in England, or Snowdonia in Wales presents difficulties for farming. Describe some of those difficulties found on both the valley floors and the higher land.

[6]

8 What word describes a piece of land that is surrounded on three sides by bodies of water, in South Korea's case, seas? Tick **one**.

Peninsula ☐

Insula ☐

Archipelago ☐

Tombolo ☐ [1]

Progress Test 4

9 Following long periods of continuous heavy rain during the winters of 2019–2020, many areas of the UK flooded. A number of strategies to help prevent future flooding have been suggested. Three of these are:

- put meanders back into rivers that have been straightened
- plant trees in river catchment areas
- restrict house building on river floodplains.

Choose **one** of these and explain how it could help reduce the likelihood of flooding in the future.

Chosen strategy ....

Explanation ....

....

....

....

....   [4]

10 The following are lists of countries. Which set are all part of the Middle East? Tick **one**.

Egypt, Turkey, India, Iraq ☐

Yemen, Saudi Arabia, Jordan, Israel ☐

Oman, Qatar, Bahrain, Greece ☐

Syria, Lebanon, Bangladesh, United Arab Emirates ☐   [1]

11 Between North America and Europe is a constructive plate margin.

a) What is this margin called? ....   [1]

b) What type of volcano is associated with this kind of margin?

....   [1]

12 What do the letters NEE stand for?

....   [1]

13 **a)** A Mediterranean climate is warm with dry summers and wet winters. It is found in countries around the Mediterranean Sea. Name **one** other place/area of the world which has a Mediterranean climate.

....   [1]

b) In Mediterranean countries such as Italy the winter rainfall is cyclonic, coming from weak depressions. What are the **two** other types of rainfall?

_____

_____ [2]

14 Which line drawn in the 1970s aimed to show the world separated into developed and developing nations?

_____ [1]

15 Look at this graph.

What is the name of this type of graph?

_____ [1]

16 Which of the following are reasons why the world's population **did not** grow rapidly until 1800? Tick **three** boxes.

Lack of medicines ☐

Low amount of crops ☐

Low birth rates ☐

Low death rates ☐

Poor medical understanding ☐

Global conflict ☐ [3]

Total Marks _____ / 43

Geography Skills

Ordnance Survey Maps

1 Complete the sentences below.

  a) Using an 8-point compass: south-east is halfway between _____ and _____, and is opposite _____ . [3]

  b) Using a 16-point compass: west-north-west is halfway between _____ and _____, and opposite _____ . [3]

2 Look at diagrams A, B, C and D below. They are contour diagrams of four landscape features.

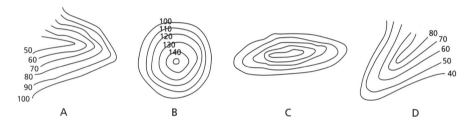

  a) Which diagram shows a hill? _____ [1]

  b) Which diagram shows a valley? _____ [1]

  c) Which diagram shows a ridge? _____ [1]

  d) i) Which diagram have you not used? _____

  ii) What landscape feature does it represent? _____ [2]

3 Look at the contour diagram below.

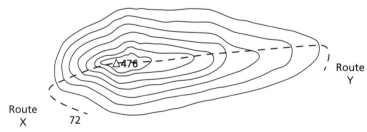

  a) How many metres of climb are there on route X, from the spot height 72 m to the highest point? _____ [1]

  b) Which is the steeper route, X or Y? _____ [1]

  c) Explain why you chose your answer to **b)**.

  _____

  _____ [1]

4 Look at the extract from the 1:50000 O.S. map 91 of Appleby-in-Westmorland shown below.

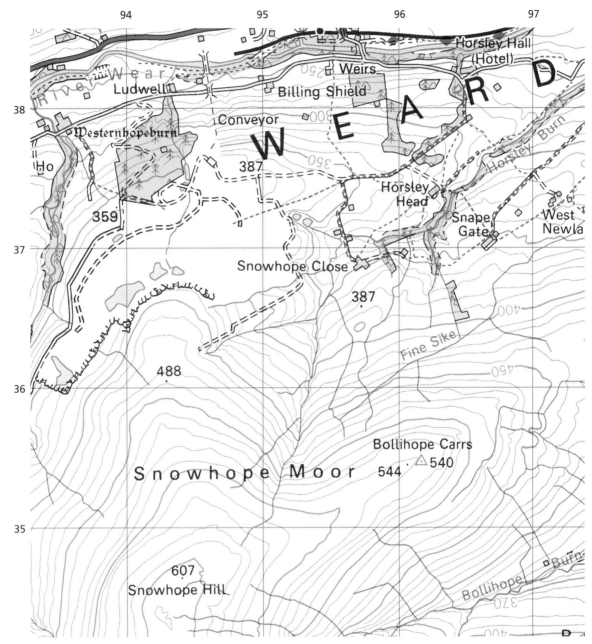

In which compass direction do the rivers in grid square 9535 flow?

_____

[1]

Geography Skills

5 Study this extract taken from O.S. map 156, Saxmundham, Aldeburgh and Southwold.

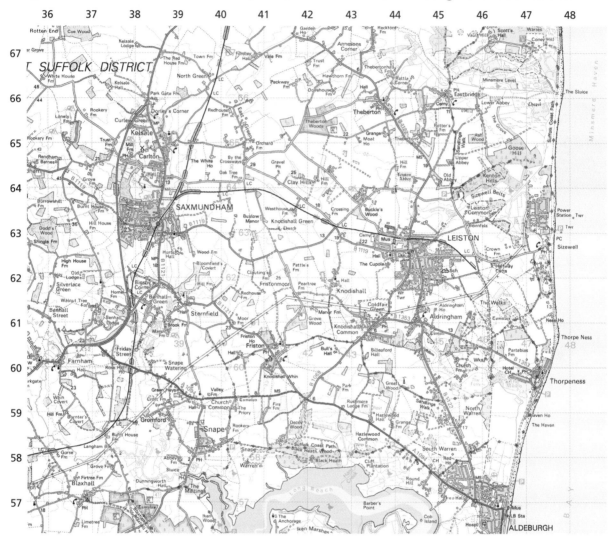

Follow the railway route from Saxmundham station (grid square 3863) to Leiston (grid square 4462).

Give a six-figure grid reference for:

a) the start of an embankment .... [2]

b) a level crossing .... [2]

6 The area shown in the O.S. map in question 5 is a popular tourist destination. What is the beach material at Thorpeness?

_____ [1]

7 Find the cycle path which goes from the B1119 west of Leiston to the A1094, south of Friston.

a) What distance would be cycled between those two points?

_____ [2]

b) Explain **one** possible hazard for a cyclist taking this route.

_____

_____

_____ [2]

c) Give **one** piece of evidence from the map that this area might suffer from flooding.

_____

_____

_____ [2]

Total Marks _____ / 26

Geography Skills

Geographic Information Systems (GIS)

1 This image is taken from part of the Defra UK (Department for Environment, Food & Rural Affairs) GIS website (https://magic.defra.gov.uk).

a) Why is the symbol to the left of the 'Table of Contents' appropriate?

_____ [1]

b) The sliders under each heading let users change the amount of transparency. Why is this a useful thing to do?

_____

_____ [2]

c) In GIS, what is meant by a 'base map'?

_____ [1]

d) This image shows the map with only 'Background Mapping' chosen.

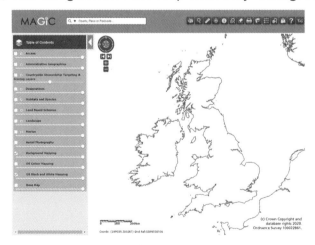

What type of information might appear if the 'Base Map' box was chosen?

_____ [1]

e) In this image, Areas of Outstanding Natural Beauty has been selected.

Explain what will happen if the ⓘ symbol next to this heading is chosen.

....

....

....

....

[2]

2 Some maps have 3D viewing available. Suggest and describe one use of a 3D view that would help understanding in physical geography.

....

....

....

[3]

3 This image is from the Met Office UK website and shows the information you can select to be shown on the map. This shows wind direction and strength.

From the list to the right of the image, select **one** type of information you would expect to be shown as coloured shading.

....

[1]

4 You are designing a story map of a visit you have made, to send to a friend. It will have three layers and pop-ups on each layer.

a) Describe your base map.

....

[1]

b) What will your three layers contain?

....

....

[3]

c) Describe the content of one pop-up and say which layer it is part of.

....

....

....

....

[4]

Total Marks .... / 19

Geography Skills

1 Information about the main shopping street in two towns has been collected. Some of the results are shown below.

Type of building	Town A	Tally	Town B	Tally
House	ⱵⱵ I		ⱵⱵ ⱵⱵ II	
Supermarket	III		II	
Clothes shop	ⱵⱵ ⱵⱵ ⱵⱵ IIII		ⱵⱵ II	
Furniture and household shops	ⱵⱵ		ⱵⱵ	
Fruit, vegetable, flower shops	III		II	
Butchers	III		II	
Bread and cakes	III		II	
Other food shops	ⱵⱵ		II	
Jeweller, gift shop	ⱵⱵ		I	

a) Complete the chart by putting the totals in the 'tally' columns. [2]

b) How would you show this type of information on a map?

....

.... [2]

c) It is decided to combine some of the shops under the heading 'food shops'.

i) Give **one** advantage of doing this.

.... [1]

ii) Give **one** disadvantage of doing this.

.... [1]

d) Some students decide to show the information on two pie charts side by side. Other students want to use vertical bars with both towns shown on the same base.

Compare the effectiveness of the two types of diagram for this information.

Pie chart   Bar chart

....

....

_____

_____

_____

_____ [6]

e) Which is likely to be the bigger town, A or B? _____ [1]

f) What is the evidence for your answer in **e)**?

_____

_____ [3]

2 A group of students want to visit the local beach to collect some data.

a) What information should be found out, and why, before a date is decided upon?

_____

_____

_____ [4]

b) Suggest and justify **one** precaution that the students should take to make sure that they are safe when working on the beach.

_____

_____ [2]

c) The students want to find out if the size of the surface material changes as you move from the cliffs towards the sea. Some of the equipment they plan to use is listed below. Choose **two** and explain how and why it would be used.

ruler	callipers	1-metre quadrat	tape measure

Equipment type _____ Description of use _____

_____

Equipment type _____ Description of use _____

_____ [4]

Progress Test 5

1 What word beginning with 'i' describes roads, sewers and electricity lines?

.... [1]

2 Sea walls have been built in many places to try to stop coastal erosion. Describe some of the characteristics of sea walls.

....

....

.... [4]

3 A class is gathering data about a river valley. In groups they are measuring the shape and occupation of stream channels.

a) Why are pupils told to work facing upstream?

....

.... [2]

b) Why is it important to avoid moving any of the material on the stream bed when taking measurements?

....

.... [2]

4 The Caspian Sea that separates Russia from Iran is actually a huge lake.

Is this statement true or false? .... [1]

5 **a)** What is a map projection?

.... [1]

b) This outline shows the Mercator map projection.

Which areas of the world have most distortion in the Mercator projection?

....

.... [1]

c) This map shows the Peters projection of the world.

What is **one** advantage of the Peters projection compared to the Mercator?

....

....

[1]

6 In which mountain range containing Mount Everest does the Brahmaputra River originate?

.... [1]

7 a) Moraine is the general term for material left behind by ice. What are the thick sheets of moraine left on valley floors and plains called?

.... [1]

b) Why do medial moraines tend to disappear after ice has retreated?

.... [1]

c) Moraine is often 'unsorted'. What does this mean?

.... [1]

8 Beneath which line do the majority of the world's lowest energy-consuming countries lie?
Tick **one**.

Brandt Line ☐   Schmidt Line ☐

Wendt Line ☐   Stein Line ☐   [1]

9 With reference to a 1:50000 O.S. map…

a) The distance between two churches measures 7.2 centimetres. What is the actual distance?

.... [2]

b) What colour are buildings in housing areas? .... [1]

c) What would you expect to see if you went to an area shown entirely plain white on the map?

.... [2]

10 What information about a country could help us to ascertain whether it has a good healthcare system? Choose from the options below.

Life expectancy ☐   The types of jobs people do ☐

Doctors per person ☐   Calorific intake ☐   [2]

11 In what ways are some UK natural environments fragile and under threat?

_____

_____

_____

_____   [4]

12 a) What do the initials GIS stand for? _____ [1]

b) What do the initials GPS stand for? _____ [1]

c) What is the link between GPS and GIS?

_____

_____   [2]

13 Which of the following countries are regarded as high-energy-using countries? Tick **two**.

United States ☐   Nigeria ☐

Peru ☐   Canada ☐   [2]

14 With reference to a 1:50000 O.S. map...

a) If contour lines are very close together, what is the landscape like? _____ [1]

b) How does the map show bare rock outcrops? _____ [1]

c) What colour are tourist features? _____ [1]

d) Green is used to show trees. In the space below, draw and label the various green tree symbols used.   [4]

15 The data below shows the main wind direction in one place for each day in March of one year. Use the figures to complete the wind rose.

Wind direction	Number of days
North	3
North East	1
East	0
South East	0
South	0
South West	14
West	7
North West	6

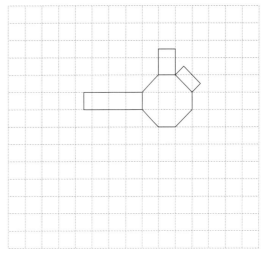

[4]

16 Which huge Asian country has experienced rapid economic development since the 1970s?

[1]

17 a) Give **two** differences between oceanic and continental crust.

[2]

b) Give **two** features that form as a result of the meeting of an oceanic and a continental plate.

[2]

18 Some pupils are planning to record wind conditions around their school site.

a) What instruments will they need? [2]

b) Suggest **two** ways they could make sure that the information collected by everyone is comparable.

[2]

c) The school site has been mapped and there is a digital version. How might the information collected about the **wind direction** in different locations be shown on the base map of the school site?

[1]

d) Some pupils want to show the **wind speed** as a figure on the same map. Give **one** positive and **one** negative for using a figure.

Positive .... [1]

Negative .... [1]

e) What would be an alternative way of showing wind speed on the map?

....

.... [2]

19 Nigeria is a low income country or LIC. Countries like Nigeria suffer from similar problems. Which of the four answers are all problems for Nigeria? Tick **one** box.

High birth rate, low national income per person, high death rate, high skills ☐

Poor roads, good healthcare, good schools, overcrowding ☐

Poor roads, poor healthcare, high birth rates, low life expectancy ☐

Pollution, terrorism, good trade, developed tourist industry ☐ [1]

20 With reference to a 1:25000 O.S. map...

a) How are 'important' buildings shown differently to other buildings? .... [1]

b) The distance between two schools is 8.4 centimetres on the map. How far is that in real life?

.... [2]

c) What is the actual distance between contour lines? .... [1]

d) Complete the table by adding the meaning or drawing the symbol.

TH	
FB	
▨	
	Triangulation pillar
	Railway cutting

[5]

e) What is the reason for a railway cutting? ....

.... [2]

21 Both flow lines and desire lines could be used to show movement between villages and a city. Compare flow lines and desire lines for this purpose.

....

.... [3]

22 What is the difference between dense population and sparse population?

....

.... [2]

23 The data collected by a group of students for a stream channel is given below. They took measurements every 50 centimetres. The water was 15 centimetres below the bank at the start.

Distance from start (cm)	Water depth (cm)
0	1
50	5
100	12
150	23
200	32
250	36
300	21
350	19
400	9
450	1

a) Draw the stream channel and water level on the frame below. Add figures and labels for axes and water surface. [5]

b) What other information should they collect in order to work out the stream discharge [amount of water passing through the channel at one time]?

.... [1]

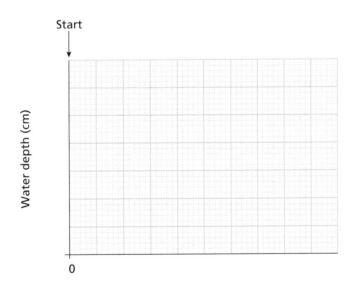

Start

Water depth (cm)

0

24 In what year did the UK's population reach 80% urbanised? Choose from the answers below.

2019–20 ☐   2005–06 ☐

2010–11 ☐   1939–40 ☐   [1]

Total Marks .... / 84

Mixed Test-Style Questions

1 Draw lines to match the following Middle Eastern countries with their capital cities.

Egypt	Damascus
Iraq	Cairo
Lebanon	Baghdad
Syria	Beirut

4 marks

2 **a)** Which soil is likely to be waterlogged, a clay or sandy soil? ....

1 mark

b) What problems does waterlogging cause for plant growth?

....

....

3 marks

3 Look at the map of Great Britain below.

☐ A   ☰ B

Underline the correct word in each sentence.

a) The rocks in areas with shading A are mainly sedimentary/metamorphic.

1 mark

b) The rocks in areas with shading B are mainly sedimentary/metamorphic.

1 mark

c) Which **two** of locations X, Y, and Z have some igneous rocks?

.... ☐

2 marks

d) How do slopes on sedimentary rocks differ from slopes on metamorphic rocks?

....

.... ☐

2 marks

4 On which of the following oceans does Nigeria have a coastline? Tick **one**.

Pacific ☐

Indian ☐

Southern ☐

Atlantic ☐   ☐

1 mark

5 The average speed of glacier movement is about 25 centimetres per day though some move much more slowly, and the fastest was recorded at over 40 metres in one day.

a) Why do some glaciers hardly move?   ☐

....   1 mark

b) What is a sudden increase in the speed of ice movement called?   ☐

....   1 mark

c) What features form as a result of the different rates of movement in the same glacier?   ☐

....   1 mark

6 What does **economic activity** mean? Choose from the answers below.

Trade ☐

Work/world of work ☐

Making things ☐

Leisure and tourism ☐   ☐

1 mark

7 **a)** What is a choropleth map?

1 mark

b) With which of the following types of information might you use a choropleth? Put a tick next to any that would be suitable.

Rainfall total in the UK	
Population change in regions of a city	
Ethnic groups in two cities	
Housing types in a town over time	
Birth rates in European countries	

4 marks

c) Suggest **one** advantage of choropleth mapping.

1 mark

8 Given its colonial history, what is the lingua franca (common language) of Nigeria despite it being the mother tongue of relatively few Nigerians? Circle the correct answer.

French

English

Spanish

Arabic

1 mark

9 A group is studying the land use on a valley side. They use random numbers to find 50 locations. They note the altitude and land use at each location.

a) What would be a useful hypothesis for this work?

1 mark

b) What is meant by 'random numbers'?

1 mark

c) The valley-side land use is classified into four groups: rough pasture or moorland; woodland; arable farming (crops); improved pasture for grazing animals. Each place is recorded with its altitude and land use.

How could the results of this data be presented?

1 mark

d) Show by a sketch what the diagram would look like.

3 marks

e) The group decide that they want to use statistics to test their work further. Their information is recorded onto a tally chart against altitude, which is in the following groups:

0–50 m   51–100 m   101–150 m

151–200 m   201–250 m

Why might these altitude intervals have been chosen?

3 marks

10 The Eastern and Western Ghats are a series of hills in the south of India. Is this statement true or false?

1 mark

11 Look at the cross-section diagrams of two rivers.

One flows faster than the other. Say which one and explain why.

River _____ flows faster.

Explanation _____

River A

River B

3 marks

12 The Thar Desert in the north-west of India separates India from which country? Choose from the list below.

Pakistan ☐

Saudi Arabia ☐

Iran ☐

Afghanistan ☐

☐
1 mark

13 a) The word 'tundra' means 'barren land'. Explain why this is a good description of tundra areas.

....

....

☐
2 marks

b) State **two** characteristics of tundra vegetation

....

....

☐
2 marks

c) Explain how some animals adapt to tundra conditions.

....

....

....

☐
4 marks

14 South Korea is a country in what is commonly referred to as the Far East. From the four lists below, choose which countries are also in this world region.

China, Japan, India, Ukraine ☐

North Korea, Thailand, Singapore, Vietnam ☐

Indonesia, Malaysia, Saudi Arabia, Australia ☐

New Zealand, Madagascar, Sri Lanka, Myanmar ☐

☐
1 mark

15 One piece of information that has been calculated is the number of people who live within 5 km of particular volcanoes.

a) Why is that information important? ....

....

☐
1 mark

b) The Michoacán-Guanajuato volcano in Mexico has almost six million people living within 5 km, the highest total in the world. Suggest some other information that would be useful alongside this number

3 marks

16 Which mountain lying over the China/Nepal border is 8848 metres in elevation? Choose from the list below.

Annapurna ☐

Popocatepetl ☐

Everest ☐

Chimborazo ☐

1 mark

17 Humans make use of many rocks, but their extraction can cause problems. Suggest some of the problems and their causes.

4 marks

18 Tick the countries that are in what could be described as Eastern Europe and from where there has been large recent migration to the UK.

Poland ☐

Romania ☐

France ☐

Germany ☐

Czech Republic ☐

Norway ☐

USA ☐

3 marks

19 Look at these diagrams of volcanoes.

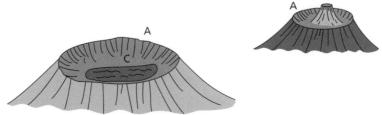

a) Both of the diagrams above have the same feature A. What is that feature?

....

1 mark

b) What is the feature labelled B? ....

1 mark

c) What is the feature labelled C? ....

1 mark

d) Explain how feature A is likely to have been formed.

....

....

....

3 marks

20 The table below shows definitions of the four types of industry. Draw lines to match up the four types to their definitions.

Manufacturing goods		Primary
Providing a service		Secondary
Research, science, technology		Tertiary
Extracting raw materials		Quaternary

4 marks

21 a) In GIS, what is meant by a polygon?

....

1 mark

b) Using examples, explain why polygons might be different shapes.

....

....

....

....

4 marks

22 The picture below shows a hand water pump being used in Bangladesh, which is a LIC.

Easy-to-use, cheap and simple-to-maintain tools such as these are known as?
Tick **one** answer.

Advanced technology ☐

Proficient technology ☐

Elementary technology ☐

Intermediate technology ☐

☐ 1 mark

23 a) Waves running up a beach is the _____.

b) Waves returning down the beach is the _____.

☐ 2 marks

24 The Yellow River forms the border of China and which other country? Choose from the list below.

North Korea ☐

South Korea ☐

Japan ☐

Australia ☐

☐ 1 mark

25 Explain in the context of weathering the difference between disintegration and decomposition.

_____

_____

_____

☐ 4 marks

26 Of the six populated continents, which continent overall uses the least energy per capita?

_____

☐ 1 mark

27 Climate and weather maps use different types of line to show places that experience the same conditions. Draw lines to match the terms with their condition.

Isobar		Temperature
Isobront		Winter temperatures
Isocheim		Precipitation
Isohyet		Wind speed
Isohel		Pressure
Isotach		Storm front
Isotherm		Sunshine hours

6 marks

28 This photograph is of a slum area in Rio de Janeiro.

Tick the problems faced by people who live in areas such as these.

Violent crime ☐

Choice of schools ☐

Poor transport links ☐

Easy access to hospitals ☐

Unemployment ☐

Good 4G signal ☐

3 marks

29 a) What are the advantages of a 1:25000 map over a 1:50000 map for a walker?

....

....

2 marks

b) What is meant by the gradient of land? ....

1 mark

c) Under the three diagrams below, draw what the contour representation would look like.

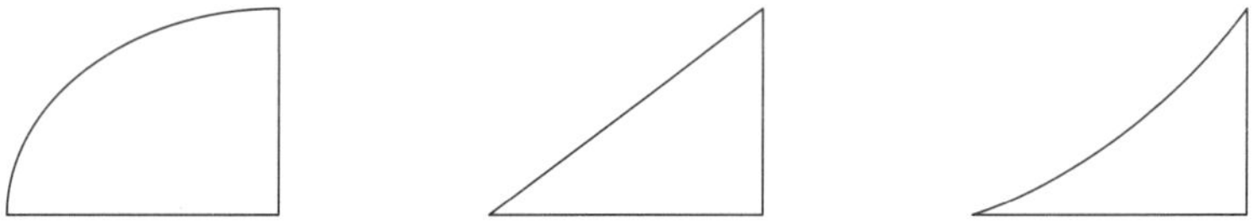

3 marks

30 The photograph in Q28 is of what Brazilian people call a *favela*. Underline the correct definition of a *favela* from the choices below.

A collection of towns and cities in a defined area.

A small town that has grown into the main city.

A squatter settlement where people do not own the land but build houses on it.

A settlement planned by the government or a charity.

1 mark

31 The soil content triangle shown below has the % of components shown. Sand is 10%.

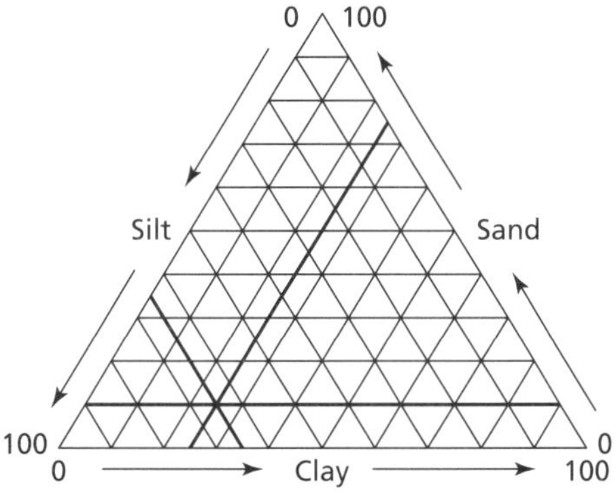

What % is clay? _____

What % is silt? _____

2 marks

32 At the end of the Permian, during the Devonian and in late Ordovician-early Silurian, there were 'mass extinctions'.

a) What is meant by 'mass extinction'?

1 mark

b) What was the likely cause of these mass extinctions? _____

1 mark

Mixed Test-Style Questions

33 Why is the sea ice to the north of Russia melting and thinning?

[ ] 1 mark

_____

34 The population pyramid below is for a low-income country.

| Male | Niger–2010 | Female |

Population (in millions)

Below are four sets of descriptions. Choose the set that best describes the pyramid.

High birth rate, high death rate, low life expectancy, high infant mortality [ ]

Low birth rate, low death rate, high life expectancy, low infant mortality [ ]

High male mortality, low female mortality, high life expectancy,
low birth rate [ ]

High life expectancy, one child policy, ageing population, high male
migration [ ]

1 mark

35 The use of which natural resource is used to compare the energy usage of different countries? Choose from the options below.

Coal [ ]

Natural gas [ ]

Oil [ ]

Water [ ]

1 mark

Answers

Pages 4–5 Location Knowledge – Russia

1. Kazakhstan, Mongolia, China **[3]**
2. Caspian Sea **[1]**
3. St Petersburg **[1]**
4. Sea of Japan **[1]**
5. Lake Baikal **[1]**
6. Any two from: Ob, Yenisey, Lena. **[2]**
7. Two well-developed statements referring to a specific river and countries for 4 marks. Simple, general statements without names or locations will gain a maximum of 2 marks. Example answers: Amur River **[1]** flows between Russia and China. **[1]** If China dammed the river and/or extracted too much water, **[1]** there could be a shortage for Russian people/cities. **[1]** Tributaries of the Ob **[1]** begin in Mongolia, China and Kazakhstan **[1]** so if they dam/extract/discharge into them, **[1]** the flow could be decreased/increased causing shortage or floods in Russia. **[1]**
8. Norway, USA, Canada, Iceland, Greenland (Denmark) **[5]**
9. Russia has a large ocean coastline along the **Arctic** Ocean. Unlike Antarctica there is no **land** beneath this frozen wilderness. Throughout human history this ocean has been **frozen**, making transport impossible. This means that **trade** routes for Russian produce have been much longer. However, due to **climate** change, the sea ice has thinned making passage through the ice much **easier**. **[1 mark per correct answer, up to 6 marks]**
10. Bering Sea or Chukchi Sea **[1]**
11. Canada **[1]**

Pages 6–7 Location Knowledge – China

1. Any three from: Kyrgyzstan, Kazakhstan, Pakistan, Tajikistan, Afghanistan, Mongolia, Russia, India, Pakistan, Vietnam, Laos, Myanmar, Nepal, North Korea, Bhutan. **[3]**
2. Yellow Sea **[1]**
3. South China Sea **[1]**
4. Taiwan Strait **[1]**
5. Macao or Hong Kong **[1]**
6. Yangtze, Yellow **[2]**
7. Any two from: Building cities along the coast means trade is easier. Building cities along the coast means transport is easier. Coastal areas tend to be lowland therefore building cities is easier. Lowland coastal areas tend to have more temperate climates. River valleys are often flat therefore easier to build on. Rivers are a source of fresh water and/or food. Rivers provide excellent transport routes. **[2]**
8. Mekong **[1]**
9. Gobi **[1]**
10. Plateau of Tibet/Kunlun Shan **[1]**
11. Everest **[1]**
12. Gongga Shan **[1]**
13. Brahmaputra **[1]**
14. East **[1]**
15. Yalu River **[1]**

Pages 8–9 Location Knowledge – India

1. Any three from: Pakistan, Bangladesh, Bhutan, China, Nepal, Myanmar. **[3]**
2. Bay of Bengal **[1]**
3. Arabian Sea **[1]**
4. Narmada River **[1]**
5. Calcutta/Kolkata **[1]**
6. Any two from: Ganges, Brahmaputra, Mahanad, Godavari, Krishna, Kaveri. **[2]**

7. The countries associated with the rivers need to be named and something specific about them stated. As the major rivers rise in the Himalayas, there could be reference to spring snow melt/winter lower flow due to freezing which could be made worse if different countries abuse the rivers. Example answer, any four points from: Brahmaputra flows through China, India and Bangladesh **[1]** providing water for drinking, irrigation, power to all countries. **[1 mark for any country named]** It is also important for ships/navigation between the countries. **[1]** If one country changes the flow/damages water quality/extracts more than usual **[1 mark for any of these points]** it could have a serious impact on countries downstream. **[1]**

8. Any three from: Anai Mudi, Dapha Bum, Kangto, Nunkun, Sandakphu Peak, Shaluni, Shilla, Takpa Shiri. **[3]**

9. Himalayas **[1]**

10. Thar Desert **[1]**

11. Deccan **[1]**

12. Anai Mudi **[1]**

13. Mahendragiri **[1]**

14. Indian Ocean **[1]**

Pages 10–11 Location Knowledge – The Middle East

1. Any three from: Yemen, Oman, United Arab Emirates, Iraq, Kuwait, Jordan, Qatar. **[3]**

2. Mediterranean **[1]**

3. Any three from: Turkey, Georgia, Russia, Ukraine, Romania, Bulgaria. **[3]**

4. 30° North **[1]**

5. Tropic of Cancer **[1]**

6. Yemen **[1]**

7. Turkey, Syria, Iraq **[3]**

8. The countries and areas in the map above are commonly referred to as the **Levant**. These countries and areas have been the sites of much **conflict** throughout the centuries. Jordan, Egypt, Syria, Iraq and Saudi Arabia are majority **Muslim** countries. Israel, set up officially after the **Holocaust** of the Second World War, is a majority **Jewish** state. Lebanon and Cyprus both have sizeable **Christian** communities, which in Lebanon's case live happily alongside their Muslim countrymen but in Cyprus they live in **separate** parts of the country. **[1 mark per correct answer, up to 7 marks]**

9. Any two from: West Bank, Gaza, Golan Heights. **[1]**

10. Mediterranean **[1]**

11. Any two sensible points but better if locations are mentioned. Example: Turkish dams control water flow which could lead to water shortages in Syria **[1]** especially a problem as this is an arid/dry region. **[1]** Building on/near rivers could cause pollution of the water. **[1]** Drinking water and/or fish will be badly/negatively affected. **[1]** **[2]**

Pages 12–13 Location Knowledge – Nigeria

1. Cameroon, Benin, Niger **[3]**

2. Niger **[1]**

3. Lokoja **[1]**

4. Benue **[1]**

5. Lake Chad **[1]**

6. **a)** Kano
   b) Okbomoshu
   c) Oyo
   d) Uyo **[4]**

7. South **[1]**

8. The Niger **Delta** is found at the mouth of the river where it meets the sea known as the **Bight** of **Bonny**. Landforms like these are found at the **coast** and are where a river slows down and drops **sediment** that it has carried. They then split into smaller channels known as **distributaries**. The soil in these landforms, known as **alluvium**, is rich and fertile, making it excellent for **farming**. **[1 mark per correct answer, up to 8 marks]**

Pages 14–15 Location Knowledge – South Korea

1. North Korea, Japan, China [3]
2. Yellow Sea [1]
3. Seoul [1]
4. Jejudo [1]
5. East China Sea [1]
6. Ulleungdo [1]
7. Sea of Japan [1]
8. Nakdong-gang (Nakdong River) [1]
9. Geum-gang (Geum River) [1]
10. Han-gang and Bukhan-gang (Han and Bukhan Rivers) [1]
11. 1915 metres [1]
12. 1708 metres [1]
13. South Korea is a small country in eastern **Asia**. It is a **peninsula**, meaning it is bordered on three sides by **water**. It is a **mountainous** country with lowlands found in the **south**. South Korea's biggest upland area, known as the **Taebaek** mountains, are found in the far **north** east, close to its border with North Korea. **[1 mark per correct answer, up to 7 marks]**

Pages 16–19 Progress Test 1

1. Any one from: India, Nepal, Bhutan, Russia, Myanmar, Laos, Vietnam, North Korea, Mongolia, Kazakhstan, Kyrgyzstan. [1]
2. Any two from: Being on the coast makes trade easier. Being on the coast facilitates the movement of people. Being on the coast tends to make cities more multicultural. [2]
3. Any three from: soil erosion, out migration, low temperatures, difficulty trading, hard to grow crops, hard to raise animals, communication difficulties, earthquakes. [3]
4. Islands [1]
5. Any one from: Bangladesh, Pakistan, China, Nepal, Bhutan, Myanmar. [1]
6. Challenges: air pollution, high land values, social isolation, close to hostile neighbouring country, traffic congestion.

Opportunities: job opportunities, choice of lifestyle, excellent transport links. [8]
7. Floods; tropical storms [2]
8. Any three from: overcrowding, disease, malnutrition, lack of sanitation, unemployment, poor quality housing, poor transport, poor air quality leading to bronchial conditions/asthma, prejudice. [3]
9. Black Sea [1]
10. Any three from: Egypt, Saudi Arabia, United Arab Emirates, Oman. [3]
11. Any one from: Chad, Benin, Niger, Cameroon. [1]
12. The point where two rivers meet. [1]
13. Any two from: illegal migrants may use the river to get into Nigeria; Cameroon could disrupt the flow of the river; Cameroon could dam the river; Cameroon could pollute the river. [2]
14. A piece of land [1] surrounded on three sides by water. [1]
15. North Korea [1]
16. Japan [1]
17. Europe [1] and Asia [1]
18. Any two from: oil, minerals, transport, tourism, security. [2]
19. West [1]

Pages 20–27 Physical Geography

Pages 20–21 Geological Timescale

1.

Period	3
Age	5
Eon	1
Epoch	4
Era	2

[1 mark per correct answer up to a maximum of 4 marks] [4]

2. a) Any one from: fossils; radiometric dating/radioactive element decay; observing nearby sediments. [1]

b) Faulting, especially thrust faults **[1]**; folding with later surface erosion. **[1]**

3. **a)** Not all the time periods are the same length and it is important to show the huge range. **[1]**

b) Humans next to quaternary. **[1]**

c) Tertiary – mammal; Cretaceous – ammonite; Permian – reptile; Devonian – fish; Ordovician – coral; Cambrian – trilobite.
[1 mark per correct answer up to a maximum of 5 marks]

4. The marking for this question is flexible and generous. If the answer picks out which bit of the planetary system (s) is affected and some idea of the nature of the damage (d) and/or cause, the full 3 marks will be given (see example given for Paper Production, below). Answers should explain how the human activities chosen have an impact on any aspect of the planet system (land, atmosphere, water, vegetation) so that the term 'Anthropocene' is appropriate. Any two from:

Paper Production: Affects water, vegetation and land. Paper is in increasing demand. Countries are under pressure to cut down forests/plant non-native trees to meet the demand. This affects the other plants/animals and soil, (d) leading to loss of ecosystems. (d/s) Over 50% of all paper and card is used for packaging. This creates a problem of waste. (d) Paper production consumes a huge amount of water and can cause water pollution. (d) **[3]**

Tropical Forest Loss: Affects land, water, atmosphere, vegetation. Forests are essential to the way Earth operates. They are home to a huge variety of plants and animals, **[1]** control weather systems, **[1]** and absorb carbon dioxide. **[1]** Their loss makes climates drier **[1]** and if more than a certain amount is lost, their whole system will collapse. **[1]** **[Up to a maximum of 3 marks]**

Water Use: Demand for fresh water is greater than population growth because water is used for agriculture and industry. Rivers are not able to supply the demand so people are extracting water from deep underground/fossil water which takes a very long time/thousands of years to replace. **[3]**

Primary Energy Use: Use of fossil fuels/coal and gas enabled industrial development. Their extraction increased other extractions (metals etc). Impacts are on the land through mining and waste production, deforestation and transport; on air through emissions of greenhouse gases. **[3]**

Domesticated Land: There is very little truly wild/natural/original landscape left on Earth as so much is used for farming/agriculture. This means that the soils have been changed and erosion of landscapes increased/changed. Use of chemicals in farming can damage soils and pollute water systems. **[3]** **[6]**

Pages 22–23 Plate Tectonics

1.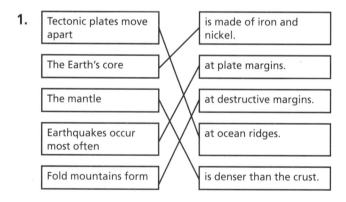

[1 mark for one correct; 2 marks for two correct; 3 marks for three correct; 4 marks for four or five correct]

2. Key to answering this question is showing where the molten rock comes from/is formed, and how it is able to rise to the surface. Plate type/movement is critical. There's no need to give example(s). No mark will be given

for identification of location type. Three separate points to be made including one which must be for plate situation.

Location A: In fold mountains

Reason for volcanoes: One plate dips/subducts/is pulled below another less dense one/oceanic plate is pulled or subducted beneath a continental plate. **[1]** Plate material melts at higher temperatures below surface/in mantle. **[1]** Less dense ('lighter' would be allowed) material rises to surface. **[1]**

Location B: Mid-ocean ridges

Reason for volcanoes: Plates move apart/diverge **[1]** allowing molten rock/magma to rise **[1]** to the surface and form submarine volcanoes. **[1]**

Location C: Hot spots

Reason for volcanoes: Above magma plumes/particularly hot areas. **[1]** Molten rock rises through cracks in rocks. **[1]** Not often related to plate boundaries. **[1]**

Location D: Island arc

Reason for volcanoes: When two oceanic plates meet, **[1]** the older/denser plate subducts beneath the younger/less dense plate. **[1]** Plate material melts and rises to form volcanic islands. **[1]**

3. A discursive answer is needed. Any reasonable ideas can be credited. No marks will be given for any notion of the 'strength' of the explosion. There may be useful examples cited, e.g. no deaths from lava or ash with initial eruption of Paracutin, which appeared in a field in 1943, but three people died from associated lightning strikes.

Any from: nature of material being ejected – lavas can be less dangerous than gases, ash, tephra/molten lumps of rock; mudflows/lahars under snow-capped volcanoes cause especially high fatality numbers; eruptions in sparsely populated/densely populated regions affecting the number of potential victims; warnings; preparedness of a population; communications; ease of evacuation. **[Any 3 marks x 2 for detailed ideas; or 3 x 2 marks for three less detailed ideas]**

4.

    [12]

Pages 24–25 Rocks and Geology

1. a) Any correct example for each type, e.g. Igneous: basalt; granite; pumice. Sedimentary: limestone; chalk; sandstone. Metamorphic: slate; gneiss; marble. **[1 mark per correct example up to a maximum of 3 marks]** **[3]**

    b)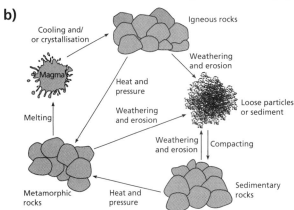

        [1 mark per correct label up to a maximum of 7 marks] **[7]**

2. a) A rock that allows water to pass into **[1]** and through **[1]** it. **[2]**

    b) Diagram should show passageways **[1]** through the rock, in between solid 'dry' areas **[1]**; not spaces holding water.

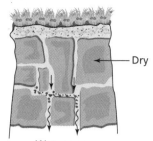

Water passes
between dry areas/in spaces between

3. a) C [1]
    b) Snow melts in spring [1] and carries
       material down to the lake where it
       sinks to the bottom. [1] Rivers erode
       material from the channel [1] and carry
       it/transport it [1] down to the lake.
       Could include reference to rainwater
       or groundwater movement taking
       sediment into the lake. [Only 1 mark for
       the sinking of sediment/particles will be
       allowed, however often it is repeated.]

4. a) Magma/volcanic material rises and
       flows between (intrudes) the layers of
       sedimentary rock [1]; cools/hardens. [1]
       [Must indicate origin of material and
       relationship to surrounding area.]
    b) Igneous rock (may say intrusions) more
       resistant/harder than surroundings. [1]

Pages 26–27 Weathering and Soil

1. a) C [1]
    b) Frost cracking/shattering needs
       temperatures to be above and below [1]
       freezing and some available water. [1]
    c) A [1]
2. a) Water [1]
    b) i) A [1]
       ii) Lots of water [1] to keep chemical
           reactions happening [1]/higher
           temperatures [1] which make most
           chemical reactions more effective/
           quicker [1] [1 mark for factor, 1 mark
           for explanation up to a maximum of
           2 marks]
       iii) C [1]

3. The point of this question is to link the
    weathering processes with landscape. Look
    for any relevant type of weathering linked
    to a feature on the field sketch.
    For example: Deep chemical weathering
    when this area was not exposed weakening
    rock, especially along joints and/or bedding
    planes. [2] Removal of surface material
    over time means the pressure is lifted off
    the rock so the rock layers spring apart/
    open up. [2] Exfoliation/removal of rock
    in sheets [1] with temperature change
    and rainfall. [1] Vertical weaknesses/cracks
    in the rock can be opened up/exploited
    by rain action/frost action/plant roots.
    [2] [Credit will be given for reference
    to mechanical weathering indicated by
    unchanged rocks/boulders which are
    broken but not altered.] [Up to a maximum
    of 4 marks]

4. a) A is well mixed [1] organic and fully
       weathered mineral material [1] but
       B has little organic material [1] and is
       almost all mineral material [1] but which
       has been weathered [1] [The comparison
       needs to be clear so 1 + 2 or 2 + 1 for
       full marks up to a maximum of 3 marks]
    b) Bedrock/parent material/unaltered rock.
       [Any one for 1 mark]
    c) Main influences are: Soil texture [1] as
       different rocks weather to different
       grain sizes. [1] Soil depth [1] as some
       rocks/harder/more resistant rocks very
       slow to weather. [1] Soil water retention
       [1] as permeable rock allows water to
       pass through/impermeable rock will stop
       water passing through. [1] [This question
       links weathering directly to soil. Any
       relevant idea that is qualified will be
       awarded marks. Only one influence is
       asked for so only credit one idea with its
       explanation for a maximum of 2 marks]

Pages 28–31 Progress Test 2

1. Farmers [1]

2. a) Algae; Corals; Fish; Amphibians;
      Birds **[1 mark for each correct answer up
      to a maximum of 4 marks]**

   b)
Characteristic	Ocean or desert?
Dark red	D
Contains fossils	O
Contains salt	D
Found with limestones	O

   **[1 mark for each correct answer up to a
   maximum of 3 marks]**

3. Any two from: fishing industry; water for
   irrigation; tourism industry; fresh water;
   easily defendable border; potential for
   hydro-electric power. [2]

4. a) Very weak/no damage/not noticed by
      humans. [1]

   b) Magnitude is physical strength/amount
      of shaking **[1]** whereas intensity is about
      the impact on humans. **[1]**

   c) Magnitude is a logarithmic scale/has no
      limits **[1]** whereas intensity scale goes
      from 1 to 10 or 12. **[1]** [There are two
      versions in use by different organisations
      and books so either will be accepted.]

5. Ploughing will compact the soil/compress
   pores/spaces **[1]**, which means that air and
   water cannot pass though **[1]**, preventing
   root development. **[1]**

6. Any one from: increased opportunities for
   trade; fishing industry; easy transport. [1]

7.
Map letter	Geological time period
B	Cretaceous
A	Jurassic
E	Triassic
C	Carboniferous
D	Devonian
F	Cambrian

   **[1 mark for each correct answer up to a
   maximum of 5 marks]**

8.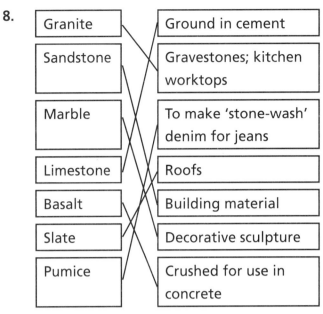

   **[1 mark for each correct answer up to a
   maximum of 6 marks]**

9. Any two from: flat land is easier to build
   on; flat land is easier to grow crops on;
   flat land is easier to raise animals on; flat
   land tends to be more fertile as there is
   less mass movement; deeper soil; ease of
   building communications. [2]

10. a) Gemstones are only found in older/
       ancient rocks. [1]

    b) Metamorphic [1]

11. a) C [1]

    b) A [1]

    c) Any three from: gas; steam; ash; lapilli;
       scoria; pumice; dust; incandescent
       fragments/nuée ardente; cinders. [3]

12. Second World War [1]

13.
Gravel	3
Cobble	2
Sand	4
Boulder	1

   **[1 mark for each correct answer up to a
   maximum of 3 marks]**

14. Any one from: Azerbaijan, North Korea,
    China, Mongolia, Kazakhstan. [1]

15. a) Activity/phenomena associated with
       earthquakes. [1]

    b) Any two from: ground shaking;
       liquefaction; fault break or slip. [2]

16. Calcutta [1]
17. a) North-west Scotland [1]
    b) Metamorphosed [1] by heat and or pressure. [1]
    c) White areas more resistant/harder than the sandstone. [1]
    d) Quartz [1]
18. Asian Tigers [1]
19. The removal of soil from the surface. [1] ['Removal of soil nutrients' would also be awarded 1 mark.]
20. Challenges: very high temperatures, little will grow, little access to clean water, conflict with neighbouring country, little transport infrastructure.
    Opportunities: tourism, long growing season, mineral deposits. [8]

Pages 32–41 **Physical Geography**

Pages 32–35 Weather and Climate

1. In January, the isotherms generally run from **north** to south. The sea tends to be **warmer** than the land. Temperatures in **north-west** Scotland are similar to those in south-east England. The **lowest** temperatures are along the North Sea coast.
    In July, temperatures increase towards the **south**. Isotherms run from **west** to east and bend north over **land** showing that the sea is **cooler** than the land. The highest temperatures are in the **south-east** of England. [**1 mark per correct answer**] [9]

   b) Influences: latitude; altitude; nearness to coast/sea; ocean currents. [1]
      Example answer: The sea moderates/ evens up temperatures [1] so coasts are warmer in winter and cooler in summer than inland areas. [1] [Alternatively, for the second mark, you could write that inland places are more extreme as too far from the sea.] [**1 mark for identification, 2 marks for explanation**]
3. a) Under 625 mm [must have unit to gain mark] [1]
   b) South or east [1]
   c) West facing/facing Atlantic [1] so receives rain from depressions/cyclonic rain events which form over Atlantic. [1] or Lots of high land/mountains [1] so relief/orographic rain forms. [1] [**Maximum of 2 marks**]
4. a) Bars do not need to be shaded. Temperature points must be joined freehand to the rest of the chart. [**1 mark per accurate plot up to a maximum of 4 marks**]
   b) 5 [1]
   c) Average/mean suggests a similarity throughout the year [1] and no indication of wet and dry seasons/times of year. [1]
   d) P [1]
5. Statements need to refer to both charts to pick out differences or similarities.
   Example answer: Five of the coolest years were over 100 years ago/in the 19th century [1] whereas the hottest years

2. a)

Description	Mild winters, warm summers	Mild winters, cool summers	Cold winters, cool summers	Cold winters, warm summers
Region (letter)	D	A	B	C

[1 mark for one correct; 2 marks for two correct; 3 marks for three or four correct] [3]

are all in the last 20 years/in the 21st century. **[1] [2 marks for this simple comparison]** The third mark will be given for a comparison illustrated with data that has been manipulated, e.g. Hottest years all within 16 years of each other **[1]**/coolest years are spread over 78 years. **[1]**

6. **a)** Answers must refer to changes to system not impacts, which are covered in **b)**. Appropriate answers will be about: changes to ocean currents; extreme weather; warming oceans; rising sea levels; oceans becoming more acidic; water cycle changes. [Two ideas should be covered with some explanation of the link to rising temperatures for full marks. If just a list, maximum 2 marks. No credit for impact.] **[6]**

    b) Drawing/diagram that focuses on the chosen impact, e.g. dying trees; an evil looking insect; lines of stick people. **[1]** Statement that picks up on the impact **[2]**, e.g. 'warmer temperatures mean insect pests can live in more areas of the world'/'more droughts mean harvests fail so people leave their home areas'. Other likely impacts are: food insecurity; forest fires; more human conflict; more animal migration; risk to water supplies; forest death; increased area of insect pests; human migration. [The design should draw attention to the impact, and wording needs to be concise and easily understood by younger children.]

Pages 36–37 Glaciation

1. **a)** The line should be below the angular section, above any rounded surface.

[1]

b) Areas above the ice will be weathered/exposed to frost **[1]** so will become jagged/more rugged as pieces break away. **[1]** [May say that below the ice, land surface can be protected or smoothed.] **[1 mark for that idea, maximum of 2 marks available]**

2. Examples: Corrie lakes are found at altitude/in the mountain, **[1]** whereas ribbon lakes are on valley floors **[1]**; corrie lakes are in rock basins **[1]** but ribbon lakes are on valley floors **[1]**; corrie lakes are usually quite circular **[1]** whereas ribbon lakes are long and thin **[1]**. [It's important to get the comparison for both marks.] **[Maximum of 2 marks]**

3. Fast-flowing rivers on the steep slopes **[1]** have brought down material/alluvium which has been deposited/left behind **[1]** as the rivers slow down on the valley floor/when entering the lake. **[1]** [A mark is also possible for making the point that the material built up most easily in shallower or calmer parts of the lake.] **[Maximum of 3 marks]**

4. Wearing away **[1]** and taking in/away **[1]** of material by moving ice. [Very important to get the idea of material being broken/worn and also removed. No need for specific types of erosion to be described but if they are, ensure that quarrying/plucking does not suggest that the ice can tear lumps of rock away.]

5. River valleys are generally V-shaped **[1]** whereas glaciated valleys are U-shaped/trough-like. **[1]**

6. Examples: Rock climbing **[1]** because ice action has made the sides steeper/more rugged (**not** higher). **[1]**

Gorge walking/ghyll scrambling/canyoning [1] in tributaries in hanging valleys. [1] Kayaking/canoeing/sailing [1] on the lakes which were created after the ice retreated/thawed. [1]
Mountain walking [1] will be given credit as long as some reference to the dramatic scenery is made. [1] [Maximum of 2 marks]

7. Differences need to be directly related to conditions necessary for ice formation and accumulation over time. Explanation of the connection to glaciers needed for the second mark in each case.
Examples: Much higher levels/amounts of snow [1] than today because snow compacts to form glacier ice. [1]
Much colder/much lower temperatures throughout the year [1] so that snow does not melt/is able to gather/accumulate [1] from year to year. [4]

8. a) Important to get the general idea that what we see today in places like the Lake District is a managed environment. People have lived in the Lake District for thousands of years and make changes continually. There is, for example, very little ancient woodland left because of farming practices. This could be a general point or specifically referring to buildings, villages, towns etc. [Any answer which indicates understanding will be awarded the maximum 2 marks]

b) Any users of the lake might consider their activities compromised, e.g. dinghy sailors might find mooring lines get in their way. Conservationists will be concerned about impact on water quality from possible houseboat waste disposal and the knock-on impact on fish and other wildlife. Could refer to erosion of lake banks as the boats will be moving. Residents may consider the boats an eyesore and noisy. Any point

should be related to a group or groups of people and explained. [3]

Pages 38–39 Rivers and Coasts

1. a) Height above sea level/altitude of source. [1]
   b) Waves [1]
   c) Moving the water along/overcoming the friction of the channel. [1]
   d) With high water/in flood. [1]
   e) Increased/heavy rainfall adds water into the channel/increases the river flow so energy is available for erosion and transport. [2] Stronger winds/storms cause bigger waves to attack the coast. [2] [Key ideas are rainfall for rivers and wind for the coast – only 2 marks for each.]

2. a)

Feature	Letter
Meander	C
Source	A
Mouth	D
Confluence	B

[4]

   b) Watershed/edge or perimeter of drainage basin. [1]
   c) Example answer: More tributaries on higher land, steeper slopes, more impermeable rock, more vegetation. [1] Fewer on gentle slopes, permeable rock, less vegetation. [1] [No credit will be given for different rainfall amounts as the drainage basin will all be in the same weather area.]
   d) Estuary [1]; delta [1]
   Descriptions: An estuary is a tidal outlet to the sea/sea water comes into the lower reaches of the river at high tide/river levels change with high and low tides. [1] Deltas form where the river divides into smaller branches/distributaries before it enters the sea/river moves in multiple channels across an area of deposited

material. [1] [Any ideas which show understanding of the situations.]

3. a) Must use/manipulate the data to get both marks. Erosion speeding up/getting worse/more dramatic. [1] Average 1 metre per year from 2005 to 2015 then 2 metres per year for five years afterwards/2015–2020. [1]

    b) Wave attack [1] undercutting the base/foundations [1]/destructive waves [1] dragging away the material under the lighthouse. [1] [Maximum of 2 marks]

    c) Any reasonable ideas that express positive and negative views should be expressed. Does not need to be restricted to this case or style of protection. Both pro and anti views must be covered to get all the marks but do not need to be balanced. A discursive approach is expected.
    Pro views: the following example paragraph of positive views has easily enough detail for 4 marks so could be a part of an answer that has a weaker 'negative' section: Coastal protection means that not just land is saved. [1] Buildings which may be used for industry or tourist attractions, which provide jobs [1] and an income to the local area, which would be lost. [1] Some houses are next to the sea. If they are not protected, people will lose their homes [1] and those quite close to the sea may be unable to get insurance. [1]
    Anti views: the following paragraph of negative views has enough detail for 4 marks so could be part of an answer that has a weaker 'positive' section: Coastal protection is considered ugly/an eyesore [1] by many because it often uses material that is not local to the area [1] so does not 'fit in'. Structures such as walls/revetements/gabions have hard lines and shapes [1] that stand out against the

landscape. [1] All protection is expensive and needs maintenance; [1] money which the local area might not be able to afford. [1] Protection in one place often leads to greater erosion along the coast [1] and can also interfere with habitats of plants and animals. [1] [Maximum 6-mark split should be 3 + 3, 4 + 2/2 + 4 so that answers have some balance]

Pages 40–41 Landscapes

1. a)
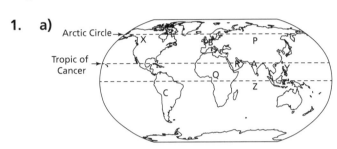

    [1 mark for each correctly drawn line of latitude]

    b) i) Country X: Canada [1]
       ii) Country Y: Japan [1]
       iii) Ocean Z: Indian [1]

2. a) B [1]; C [1]; A [1]. Even if the places are unfamiliar, use the clues: A is nearest the Equator so should be warmest; B is close to the British Isles so should look for similar characteristics; C is south of the Equator so the summer will be when British Isles has winter.   [3]

    b) Q [1]; R [1]; P [1]   [3]

3. a) The key to this question is lack of any disturbance over a very long time so that the vegetation has developed perfectly without damage. The soils are very poor so do not make any comments suggesting otherwise.
    Vegetation takes a very long time to develop and be in balance with its environment [1] but is easily disturbed by tectonic change/mountain building [1], which has not happened here. Ice ages wipe out all living things [1] but there have been none for millions of

years. There has been time for a plant/ some plants to adapt to every variation of climate/weather/soil/surface/slope **[1]** so even small changes in any of these will have caused individual species to develop. **[1] [Maximum of 4 marks]**

b) Building/urbanisation on the land which means some species may be covered over. **[1]** Water/air pollution from human activities such as farming or industries could kill the plants. **[1]** Introduced species of both plants and animals which change the food chains/ environment and threaten the natives. **[1]** Climate change which could make this area drier or hotter or have storms. **[1]** Increased dryness from climate change could lead to fires which could destroy/eliminate plants. **[1]** [Answer should suggest threats and their possible impact; threats are the same as almost everywhere else.] **[Maximum of 4 marks]**

4. a) i) Steep cliffs/coastal cliffs/gentle slope above steep cliffs **[1]**
   ii) Undulating **[1]**
   iii) High mountains/mountainous/very steep mountains **[1]**

b) Any relevant challenge(s) to humans: should indicate the issue and type of impact; on settlement, farming, communications, etc. Only one of the landscapes needs to be dealt with and as the questions says 'challenges' two are needed for 2 marks. Examples: Eroding coast threatening settlement/ disappearing land; salt affecting soils; no obvious landing area for sea transport/ no obvious access to shore; onshore winds blowing away soil.
Difficult to defend; possibly heavy soils for farming; lack of flat land for farming.

Little/no flat land for settlement or farming; communications difficulties over steep slopes; cold/snow so inhospitable for humans; steep slopes prevent soil formation. **[Maximum of 2 marks]**

Pages 42–47 Progress Test 3
1. Bangladesh **[1]**
2. a) In sediments **[1]**; underwater/sea, lakes **[1]**
   b) Any two from: teeth, shells, bones. **[2]**
   c) Provide a record of how creatures/life forms evolved/developed/became more complex **[1]**; how our separate continents were once connected **[1]**; how climate/ vegetation/environments have changed through geological time. **[1]**
3. Laos **[1]**
4. Cairo **[1]**
5. a) Polished surfaces caused by abrasion/ erosion **[1]** by particles embedded in the base of the ice which acts like sandpaper/ scours the surface. **[1]** Ruggedness caused by plucking/quarrying **[1]** which relies on frost weathering/freeze-thaw action which enables moving ice to pull out loose fragments of rock. **[1]**
   b) Striations **[1]**
6. Threats from terrorists, Poor-quality pipeline infrastructure **[2]**
7. a) The rainfall total is based on an average year taken over very many years and a month is 'any' month, not the specific one. **[1]**/Based on long-term records, the rainfall for one-twelfth of the yearly total **[1]** fell over 24 hours/1 day. **[1] [Maximum of 2 marks]**
   b) The key idea is that it is unusual but not on a cycle, e.g. A river level so high **[1]** that data/previous records would suggest it should happen every 100 years or so. **[1]**
8. Challenges: pollution by industry, remote location, overfishing.
Opportunities: tourism, access to fresh water, high biodiversity, fishing industry. **[7]**

9. Yellow Sea [1]
10. a) North-west France is not at or near a plate boundary. [1]
   b) Earthquake waves can reach the surface more quickly [1] so greater potential for damage. [1]
   c) Eastern Turkey January 2020 or Caribbean January 2020 are best answers [1] for correct choice. Amongst the shallowest so waves get to surface quickly [1]; magnitude high at 6.7/7.7 so damage likely, plus weakening of the area/fault weakening leading to potential damage in future [1]; intensity 8/7 so there has been damage to human environment. **[1 mark for correct choice + 2 marks for two reasons]**

11. Samsung [1]
12. Adaptation should be described as in the example; up to 2 marks. Reason must match the adaptation. Any biome/environment can be used. Up to 2 marks for adaptation.
    Example: Some Boreal forest trees have needle leaves [1] (adaptation) with small surface area and/or thick/waxy coating **[1 for either idea]** (adaptation), which stops the tree losing moisture/water [1] (reason) in winter when ground is frozen so water cannot be taken up [1] (reason). **[Maximum of 4 marks]**

13. a) That conditions are unlike those of present. Coal formed at times of heat and humidity/hot and wet [1] lots of plants grew at the time that were compressed to make the coal. [1]
    b) Sea creatures held in layers of sediment [1] that became sedimentary rock. [1] The rock uplifted/formed into mountains. [1]
    c) Between the layers of sediment. [1]

14. a)

A	Scree/talus	D	Meltwater stream
B	Medial moraine	E	Surface/supra-glacial moraine [scattered rocks on ice surface would be accepted]
C	Terminal [recessional moraine would be accepted]	F	Lateral moraine

[1 mark for each correct answer up to a maximum of 6 marks]

   b) Snout [1]
15. False [1]
16. a) Faults/faulting/faults [1] [There is no change of rock type so differential erosion not relevant.]
    b) Plunge pool [1]
17. Raindrops are bigger/drizzle is composed of smaller drops of water. [1]
18. This is about hanging valleys – only 1 mark is available for using the term; description needs to be coherent and cover main ideas for 4 marks. Pre-glacial river pattern with tributaries which freeze/have small glaciers in them. [1] Main/trunk/spine river valley holds huge glacier which erodes into a deep U/tough. [1] Tributaries eroded to far less extent. [1] After ice retreat the tributary valleys are left high/confluence has been cut away [1] so the tributary river pours over the valley side as a waterfall. [1] **[1 mark for each correct answer up to a maximum of 4 marks]**
19. Bedding planes and joints act as weaknesses in rocks/form cracks [1] into which water can enter [1]/much bigger surface area for weathering processes. [1] **[1 mark for the first point and 1 mark for any other point]**
20. a) Gives no idea about shape of land/slopes/exposure/proportion of the land at or near that altitude. Any answer showing understanding of the weakness. [1]

b) Example: Range of altitude/highest and lowest/proportion at or above that height. Any reasonable suggestion. **[1]**

21. More jobs; Jobs for unskilled workers; Education and healthcare; Perception of the bright lights of the big city **[4]**

22. **a)** Arrows critical to show direction. Lines must be oblique up the beach **[1]** and perpendicular/right angles back to the water. **[1]**

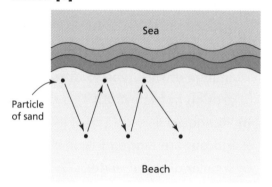

Sea

Particle of sand

Beach

   b) Longshore drift removes beach material/ some coastal places have lost their beaches altogether due to longshore drift. **[1]** Beaches part of the attraction to a resort so people would not visit/find it less attractive to visit. **[1]** [Answer must be relevant to a resort.]

23. **a)** Beaufort Scale **[1]**
   b) The wind that blows most often/ frequently. **[1]** [Not strongest, which is the dominant wind.]

24. Any two from: spit; bar; tombolo; barrier island. Not delta, which is coastal but sediment is sourced from rivers. **[2]**

25. Time zones **[1]**

Pages 48–57 Human Geography

Pages 48–49 Population

1. Population **distribution** is the study of where people live. When people live close together we call this **dense** population. When people live more spaced out we call this **sparse** population. **[1 mark per correct answer, up to 3 marks]**

2. **A** Northern Canada   dense / **sparse** **[1]**
    B Western Europe   **dense** / sparse **[1]**
    C Antarctica   dense / **sparse** **[1]**
    D Sahara Desert   dense / **sparse** **[1]**
    E India   **dense** / sparse **[1]**
    F Central Australia   dense / **sparse** **[1]**

3. Three well-developed statements for 6 marks.
   Example: Some parts of the world have a harsh climate **[1]** meaning it will be difficult for people to survive. **[1]** Some parts of the world have a dry climate **[1]** meaning it would be difficult to grow crops. **[1]** Some parts of the world have a mountainous landscape **[1]** meaning it would be hard to build homes. **[1]**

4. **a)** Lack of medicine **[1]**; Poor understanding of infectious disease **[1]**; Low amount of crops able to be grown **[1]**
   b) 125 years **[1]**

5. After World War 2 in 1945, the UK's fertility rate peaked at **2.7** babies per woman. In the mid-1960s it peaked again at about **2.9** babies. The availability of contraceptives in the 1970s led to a big **drop** in births. The rate is now between 1.7 and 1.8 because of **migration** from eastern Europe. **[4]**

Page 50 Urbanisation

1. The growth of towns and cities **[1]**
2. South America **[1]**
3. Oceania **[1]**
4. China **[1]**
5. 80% **[1]**
6. One developed statement, e.g. there will be fewer people in the countryside left **[1]** to move to the cities. **[1]**

Page 51 Urbanisation: Case study – Rio de Janeiro, Brazil

1. The *favela* lacks basic **infrastructure** like paved roads, sewers and electricity lines. The *favela* is **unplanned**, therefore there

is no control over how it has grown and developed. Population density is very **high** as people live very close together. Trust in the local police is low meaning that **crime** is difficult to control. The inhabitants of *favelas* are generally poor and have low access to good **education** and healthcare. **[1 mark per correct answer, up to 5 marks]**

2. a) People would be more likely to look after a house **[1]** not threatened with demolition. **[1]**

   b) People could improve their own homes **[1]** without government. **[1]**

   c) Cable cars would improve transport links **[1]** so employment can grow. **[1]**

Page 52 Development

1. Countries to the **north** of the line are said to be **developed** – they have a generally **higher** quality of life. Countries to the **south** of the line are said to be **developing** – they have a generally **lower** quality of life. **[1 mark per correct answer, up to 4 marks]**

2. a) USA   **developed** / developing   **[1]**

   b) Brazil   developed / **developing**   **[1]**

   c) India   developed / **developing**   **[1]**

   d) UK   **developed** / developing   **[1]**

3. b) High birth rates – these suggest poorer healthcare in a country.   **[1]**

   c) High literacy rates – this suggests better education in a country.   **[1]**

   d) Low unemployment – this suggests better education/better government/ stronger economy.   **[1]**

   e) Few older people – this suggests poorer healthcare in a country.   **[1]**

Page 53 Development: Case study – China

1. China today is the world's **second** largest economy but forty years ago it was a poor,

largely **rural** nation with at least 30% of its population living in **poverty**. In 1980 China became a member of the World **Bank**. As the economy opened up to the outside world **foreign** companies flooded into China to build factories and to take advantage of the cheap **labour** (workers). More than 500 **million** people have been lifted out of poverty since the reforms began. It's been called an economic **miracle. [1 mark per correct answer, up to 8 marks]**

2.

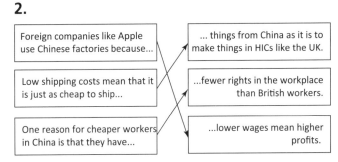

Foreign companies like Apple use Chinese factories because...

... things from China as it is to make things in HICs like the UK.

Low shipping costs mean that it is just as cheap to ship...

...fewer rights in the workplace than British workers.

One reason for cheaper workers in China is that they have...

...lower wages mean higher profits.

[3]

Pages 54–55 Economic Activity

1. Coal miner – primary   Factory worker – secondary

   Doctor – tertiary   Builder – secondary

   Artist – tertiary   Chef – tertiary

   Farmer – primary   Lorry driver – tertiary

   Postal worker – tertiary   Police officer – tertiary

   [1 mark per correct answer, up to 10 marks]

2. In the pre-industrial period, most people in the UK worked in **primary** industry, in jobs like **fishing**, **farming** and **mining**. During the industrial period, many more people became employed in **secondary** industries in jobs such as steelmaking and **ship** building. In the UK today, more people work in **tertiary** industry selling their time and skills. Jobs in today's **quaternary** industries are often in research and **technology. [1 mark per correct answer, up to 9 marks]**

3.

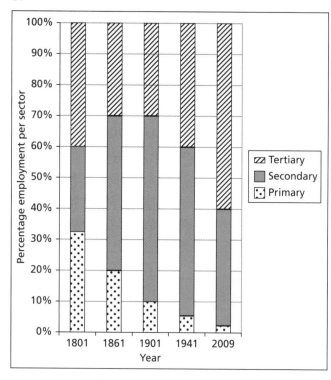

	Primary	Secondary	Tertiary
1801	33	27	40
1861	20	50	30
1901	10	60	30
1941	5	55	40
2009	3	37	60

[12] [1 mark for each correctly-placed line on the graph, up to a maximum of 12 marks]

4. Any one from: It is cheaper to produce goods abroad and ship them to the UK. Farming has become increasingly mechanised. Industries such as mining/quarrying have become more mechanised, so fewer people needed. Resources have become exhausted so mines, quarries etc. have closed. **[1]**

Pages 56–57 Natural Resources

1. Renewable: fish, wood, wheat, cattle, wind energy, solar energy, wave energy. Non-renewable: coal, oil, diamonds, limestone, natural gas. **[1 mark per correct answer, up to 12 marks]**

2. Any three from: Canada, USA, Russia, France, Germany, Kazakhstan, Australia, New Zealand, Belgium, Netherlands, Saudi

Arabia, Japan, Czech Republic, Austria, United Arab Emirates, Oman, Iceland, Norway, Sweden, Finland. **[3]**

3. The Brandt Line **[1]**

4. Any two from: a very cold climate, a very warm climate, very industrialised, high standard of living, high proportion of the population own cars, well-developed transport systems. **[2]**

5. Africa **[1]**

6. Any two from: poorly industrialised, low standard of living, low number of people own cars, poorly developed transport systems, poverty. **[2]**

7. Benefits: cheap power, creates many jobs, generates money for the country. Drawbacks: releases harmful gases, can lead to asthma in humans. **[1 mark per correct answer, up to 5 marks]**

8. Benefits: creates some jobs, releases no harmful gases, generates money for the local economy. Drawbacks: some feel it ruins the landscape, can affect migratory birds. **[1 mark per correct answer, up to 5 marks]**

Pages 58–61 Progress Test 4

1. Brazil: NEE; UK: HIC; France: HIC; Afghanistan: LIC **[4]**

2. Urbanisation **[1]**

3. 75% **[1]**; 88% **[1]**

4. Himalayas **[1]**

5.

Landscape type	Key characteristics
Remote	Away from (obvious) human influence
Rural	Dominated by countryside
Wetland	Mix of permanent and temporary water/area that gets flooded some of the time; not lakes
Moorland	Upland area that has low growing plants/heath or heathers will be allowed, and/or acid soils

[4 × 2 marks, depending on how specific the definition]

6. Renewable: a); b); d)
   Non-renewable: c) **[4]**

7. Challenges could be: terrain; weather; soil. Both upland and valley floor must be covered to gain full marks.

Higher areas: steep slopes prevent use of machinery [1]; very little/thin soil so not easy for plants to grow [1]; exposure to winds/low temperatures mean growing season is short/difficult for most animals to thrive [1]; heavy rainfall washes any nutrients from soil. [1]

Valley floor: heavy, clay soil is easily waterlogged so difficult to cultivate [1]; can be too heavy for machinery [1]; easily floods [1]; growing season short, restricting choice of crops. [1] [Mark awards of 3+3/4+2/2+4 will be allowed, up to a maximum of 6 marks]

8. Peninsula [1]

9. The chosen strategy must be explained in terms of its contribution to flood prevention. Possible themes discussed might be:

Meanders have a bigger channel area in total [1] so water has more space and can stay inside the channel for longer. [1] Meanders slow down the flow of water [1] compared to straightened channels [1] so it takes longer for extra water to move through the river system. [1] [Maximum of 4 marks available]

Trees take up water from the soil [1] so slow down the saturation of the ground [1] so rainfall falls on saturated ground less often [1] and takes longer to get into the channel. [1] Leaves and branches intercept rainfall/catch rainfall [1], which slows it down/prevents it reaching the ground. [1] Tree roots bind soil [1] and prevent it being washed into river channel [1] so the channel does not get clogged/made smaller [1] and is able to contain the rainfall. [Maximum of 4 marks available]

Buildings create more impermeable surfaces [1] which do not absorb rainfall [1] and can speed up the passage to the channel. [1] Land may be drained for building [1] so drainage pipes carry water more quickly towards channels than by natural processes. [Maximum of 4 marks available]

10. Yemen, Saudi Arabia, Jordan, Israel [1]
11. a) Mid-Atlantic Ridge [1]
    b) Fissure [1]
12. Newly Emerging Economy [1]
13. a) Any one from: South-East Australia; California; South Africa; Chile. [1]
    b) Relief/orographic [1]; convectional [1]
14. The Brandt Line [1]
15. The J Curve [1]
16. Lack of medicines; Low amount of crops; Poor medical understanding [3]

Pages 62–69 Geography Skills

Pages 62–65 Ordnance Survey Maps

1. a) South-east is halfway between east [1] and south [1], and is opposite north-west. [1]
   b) West-north-west is halfway between west [1] and north-west [1], and opposite east-south-east. [1]
2. a) B [1]
   b) A [1]
   c) C [1]
   d) i) D [1] ii) Spur [1]
3. a) 404 m [1]
   b) Route X [1]
   c) Contours on route X are closer together than on route Y *or* contours on route Y are much further apart than on route X. [1]
4. North [1]
5. a) 386634 *or* 421634 [1 mark for accurate easting and 1 mark for accurate northing

so every 6-figure reference answer gets 2 marks; a 4-figure (square) reference would get 1 mark] **[2]**

    b) 400639 (accept 399639) *or* 417636 *or* 426631 [1 mark for accurate easting and 1 mark for accurate northing so every 6-figure reference answer gets 2 marks; a 4-figure (square) reference would get 1 mark] **[2]**

6.   Shingle **[1]**

7.   a) 5.1 **[1]** km **[1]** (accept 5 km to 5.2 km, unit of distance must be included).

    b) Hazards could be: farm entrances, e.g. Pear Tree Farm (4161), Manor Farm (4261) where there may be farm vehicles turning or animals; crossing the B1121 (4161), where there could be faster traffic. Marks would also be given for turning onto the A1094, which will be carrying more and much faster traffic. Answer must identify a hazard by name or grid square location **[1]** and give a reason for the hazardous nature **[1]** of that section of route.

    c) You will not receive a mark for just writing 'low land'. The fens/marshland in 4559; drainage ditches in 4658 *or* 4653 *or* 4258. Marks will be awarded for identification of feature **[1]** and explanation given **[1]**.

Pages 66–67 Geographic Information Systems (GIS)

1.   a) Suggests layers sitting on top of each other which is how the GIS system works. **[1]**

    b) Answer needs to address both more and less transparency being available. Having more transparency makes the layers above and/or below easier to see and compare. **[1]** Having less transparency increases the focus on the specific information on that layer. **[1]**

    c) It is the setting or context for the mapped information to be seen. **[1]**

[A base map is not an outline map; some are very complex and detailed.]

    d) Boundaries of countries/counties/other regions; place names. Any appropriate answer. **[1]**

    e) Not just the term 'pop-up'. Important idea is that of an 'Information box'. **[1]** In this case an explanation of AONB, its history/function etc. **[1]**

2.   Any relevant example from physical geography (should be glaciation, rivers, coasts). Answer must suggest specifics to given example and be convincing as to benefit of 3D image, for example: glaciation example might show shapes of landforms (corries, troughs, peaks etc.) shown by contour patterns, named examples and terms used over a base map of the studied region (Snowdonia, Scottish Highlands, Lake District etc.). **[3]**

3.   Any one from: Temperature map; Rainfall; Cloud and rain; Cloud cover. **[1]**

4.   a) Type of visit unimportant except as a context. [1 mark for clear description of the base map. Location of the visit must be apparent.] **[1]**

    b) Each layer must be different and relevant to the visit. Likely to be communication/ roads and paths; settlements/towns and villages; attraction types/ views/ specific buildings etc. **[1 mark per layer up to a maximum of 3 marks]**

    c) Some detail needed for 4 marks. 1 mark for showing clearly which layer it is part of. Should always be a name/title. If a natural/landscape feature, there could be information about size, rock type, processes etc. If a building, style/age/ materials etc. A photo is an obvious inclusion. Photo of the person at the place is likely given that the end product is going to a friend. Should be 2–3 explained contents. **[4]**

1. a)

Type of building	Town A	Tally	Town B	Tally
House	卌 I	6	卌 卌 II	12
Supermarket	III	3	II	2
Clothes shop	卌 卌 卌 IIII	19	卌 II	7
Furniture and household s hops	卌	5	卌	5
Fruit, vegetable, flower shops	III	3	II	2
Butchers	III	3	II	2
Bread and cakes	III	3	II	2
Other food shops	卌	5	II	2
Jeweller, gift shop	卌	5	I	1

[I mark for each correctly completed tally column, up to 2 marks]

b) Streets shown as a single line with boxes drawn to represent each building. **[1]** Different building types given a colour/shading. **[1]**

c) i) Any one useful idea, for example: fewer categories makes mapping/plotting less confusing as fewer colours will be used **[1]**; bigger numbers and fewer groups might make numerical/statistical analysis easier. **[1]**

ii) Any one relevant point, for example: some useful information about the place could be lost **[1]**; specialist shops are found in different sorts of places and that will not be seen. **[1]**

d) Both types of diagram must be referenced with positive and negative ideas, for example: Pie charts are more complex/time consuming to draw **[1]** and need the raw data to be converted into degrees or % **[1]**, but might make picking out one particular type of building easier and will show the information about each place easier to study alone. **[1]** Joined bars are easy to draw **[1]** but if the data is very varied, finding a sensible scale could be difficult.

[1] Comparison of each type of building in the two places is very easy. **[1]**

e) A **[1]**

f) Any reasoned explanation(s). Can emphasise A being bigger or B being smaller. The choice has been made so no credit for repeating which is bigger. There are more shops in A than B (46:35) **[1]** with more specialist shops, e.g. jewellery, clothes. **[1]** These need more customers **[1]** so A is likely to be bigger. B has more houses near the shops (12:6) **[1]** which, as this is the main shopping street, **[1]** means B is likely to be a smaller place. B has almost as many 'everyday' shops, e.g. butchers but fewer specialist shops **[1]** so is likely to be smaller. **[Maximum of 3 marks]**

2. a) The most important and the only possible advance information for this fieldwork organisation is finding out the time of the tides. Time of high and low tides **[1]** to enable enough time to complete tasks on the beach **[1]** and whether it is spring tide/neap tide **[1]** to judge amount of beach available for the work **[1]**. No credit for

weather conditions, which could not be accurately forecast sufficiently far ahead.

b) Any precaution with associated justification, for example: staying away from cliff foot for any length of time [1] in case of falling material [1]; marking out the limit of work at the sea end of the beach [1] to avoid getting wet/ getting caught by a wave [1]; noting presence of wet rock areas [1] to avoid slips/falls [1]; checking the pattern of incoming waves/tide [1] to avoid getting cut-off [1]. [Maximum of 2 marks]

c) Answer must be about method [1] related to beach task. [1]
Ruler – to measure long or short axis [1] of pebbles/beach material. [1]
Callipers – to measure any axis or thickness of beach material [1] for accurate measurement of small particles. [1]
1-metre quadrat – 1-metre quadrat means that all sizes of beach material can be included in the work [1] to indicate the area where sample measurements are to be taken [1] or to ensure measurements always taken in the same size plot. [1] [Maximum of 2 marks]
Tape measure – to mark out a line between cliff and sea and ensure that measurements are taken at equal spacing. [2] [Maximum of 4 marks]

Pages 70–75 Progress Test 5

1. Infrastructure [1]
2. No credit will be given for judgement on effectiveness; the answer should be descriptive and relate to walls only. Any four from: usually made of concrete/non-local materials; at the foot of cliffs/behind the beach/along the sea front; often recurved/curved to reflect the wave energy; may have rock armour at the base for extra strength; frequently have a promenade along the top; very expensive. [4]

3. a) Looking upstream means anything in the water, branches etc., can be seen early enough. [1] Also greater awareness of the water condition so more able to stay upright. [1] [Maximum of 2 marks]

b) The work is about the channel. Its shape is created by material on the bed/ deposited material as much as by solid rock [1] so moving anything changes the conditions that have created the water situation when being measured. [1]

4. True [1]

5. a) Any idea which suggests that a projection is flattening the globe onto a map/flat surface. [1]

b) Polar regions/further north and south/ further away from the Equator. [1]

c) Peters preserves the area of land/ countries so more accurate comparisons can be made. [1]

6. Himalayas [1]

7. a) Till [1]; Boulder clay will be allowed.

b) Medial moraines are more fragile than others. Any idea that recognises the moraines are unlikely to survive the thawing process will be awarded the 1 available mark, e.g. Medial moraines collapse as ice wastes/melts [1]; medial moraine material gets washed away as ice thaws. [1]

c) The particles are mixed up/no arranging of stones/pebbles etc. by size. [1]

8. Brandt Line [1]

9. a) 3.6 [1] km [1]. Must have distance unit for second mark.

b) Pink/pale orange [1]

c) Flat [1] farmland [1]. No credit for 'nothing'.

10. Life expectancy; Doctors per person **[2]**

11. The point of this question is to indicate that the UK is as much under threat as rainforests, savannahs, etc. and that UK environments are just as important and fragile. Once lost or significantly changed, natural systems are near impossible to recreate, especially when their formation was over a long period of time and in different conditions.

Examples might be:

Ancient woodlands which developed after the last ice age have all but disappeared and will not regenerate. These and other woodlands have been cleared over centuries for building, ships, fuel and to provide farmland. Wetlands have been drained to make the land more useful to humans. Old grassland and meadows were full of different plant and animal species, but modern arable farming does not support the plants and animals. Soil erosion is much more common in the UK than people think, mainly due to removing vegetation for farming, which leaves it open to the wind. Industry has contributed to acid rain which damages vegetation and waterways so threatening the animals that live there. Chemicals used in farming can wash into rivers and poison water-living animals. Humans have introduced species of plants and animals which have led to serious reduction in native species by taking food/ introducing disease/outcompeting for light, etc. Planting of coniferous trees changes moor/heathland or hedgerow removal and so the habitat is lost.

Any ideas that indicate how easy it is for the environment to be damaged and landscape changed with lasting consequences. Any scale acceptable – whole moors to small ponds. **[Marks may be awarded 2 + 2 or one**

very clearly developed idea may gain the full 4 marks available]

12. a) Geographic Information System[s] **[1]**

b) Global Positioning System[s] **[1]**

c) GIS uses information from GPS to provide locations. **[1]** GPS feeds location information into GIS. **[1]**

13. United States; Canada **[2]**

14. a) Steep **[1]**

b) Thin black hatching [Credit diagram] **[1]**

c) Blue **[1]**

d) Coniferous **[1]**; non-coniferous **[1]**; mixed wood **[1]**; orchard **[1]**

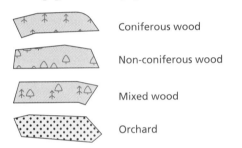

15. Bars should be drawn to scale **[2]**; two per accurate plot. **[2]** Totals are not needed on the bars; this is a visual representation which takes its impact from shape, not figures.

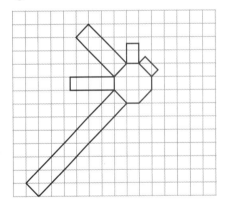

16. China [1]

17. a) Any two from: continental crust: thicker; younger; less dense; lighter coloured rocks. Could refer to oceanic. [2]

b) Not earthquakes, which are events, not features. Any two from: ocean/deep sea trench; fold mountains; volcanoes. [2]

18. a) Compass [1]; Anemometer [1]

b) Use of stopwatches which have been synchronised. [1] Using a bell/alarm at start of measurements but checking first that everyone can hear it. [1] Trialling the techniques and measurements in the classroom possibly using a fan/hairdryer. [1] Having two people working together to check each other [not more than two as more become distractors]. [1] Any two reasonable ideas that contribute to effectiveness and accuracy. **[Maximum of 2 marks]**

c) Accurately located arrows superimposed onto the base map/layer showing arrows. [1]

d) Positive: small/easy to read/does not interfere with the arrow/similar system used on some weather maps. **[Any one point for 1 mark]**
Negative: Each value needs to be read separately so no overall picture easily formed/units need to be specified, e.g. m/s or Beaufort Scale or kph/speed in figures may not be understood or accessible. **[Any one point for 1 mark]**

e) Making the arrows different thicknesses/ shading [1] getting heavier/wider/darker as speed increases. [1]

19. Poor roads, poor healthcare, high birth rates, low life expectancy [1]

20. a) A black line around the outside. [1]

b) 2.1 [1] kilometres [1]. Must have distance unit for second mark.

c) 10 metres [1]

d)

TH	Town hall
FB	Foot bridge
▨	Glasshouses
△ Blue	Triangulation pillar
⟅⟆	Railway cutting

[5]

e) Cuttings keep land for railway lines level/gentle [1] so trains do not have to climb uphill/deal with difficult terrain or gradients. [1]

21. The comparison should have both similarities and differences.
Similarities: Both are lines joining places. Both represent 'visiting' behaviour.
Differences: A desire line represents one person. Desire line maps have many lines between places but flow lines are different thicknesses, so each represents a number of people. There will only be one flow line between two places on a flow line map.
[Marks will be allocated as 1 + 2 or 2 + 1]

22. Dense population is where people live close together. [1] Sparse is where they live further apart. [1] **[1 mark for simple point, i.e. dense means close together]**

23. a) Drawing should be similar to diagram below [2]. Labels and figures with units, on both axes **[2 x 1]**.
Water level must be drawn in 15 centimetres below the bank at the left-hand side. [1]

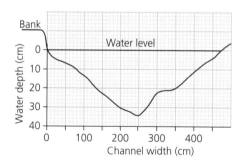

b) Speed/velocity of water at that point. [1]

24. 2005–06 [1]

Pages 76–86 Mixed Test-Style Questions

1.

Egypt	Damascus
Iraq	Cairo
Lebanon	Baghdad
Syria	Beirut

[4]

2. a) Clay [1]

b) Plant roots can find it difficult to grow into waterlogged soils. [1] Water takes the place of oxygen so plants don't get enough. [1] Plant roots cannot take in nutrients as easily when waterlogged. [1]

3. a) Sedimentary [1]

b) Metamorphic [1]

c) X and Z [2]

d) Steeper on metamorphic/gentler on sedimentary. [1] More stable/less likely to fail on metamorphic than sedimentary. [1] 'Higher' would be accepted on metamorphic.

4. Atlantic [1]

5. a) Frozen to bedrock/very cold glacier base [1]

b) Surge [1]

c) Crevasses [1]

6. Work/world of work [1]

7. a) A map which uses colours to show a range of values. [1]

b) [1 mark for each correct response: 1 = 1; 2 = 2; 3 = 3; 4/5 = 4]

Rainfall total in the UK	✓
Population change in regions of a city	✓
Ethnic groups in two cities	
Housing types in a town over time	
Birth rates in European countries	✓

c) Very easy to see/read information. [1] Extreme values stand out. [1] Gives an idea of general patterns. [1] **[Any one point for 1 mark]**

8. English [1]

9. a) 'Altitude affects land use on a valley side.' This is an example of a good answer, which must be a single, positive statement. [1]

b) Without bias [1]; not chosen by anyone [1]; generated by random number tables which are outside the influence of anyone doing the task. [1] **[Any one point for 1 mark]**

c) A scatter diagram is most appropriate. [1] It shows distribution of the land uses without assuming a relationship.

d) 1 mark for each correctly-labelled axis [2 × 1]; a further 1 mark is available for suggestion of marks in each category. [1] The number of plotted points is not important.

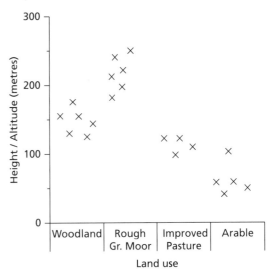

e) No overlap of values so any height can easily/clearly/accurately be plotted. [1] Manageable in terms of grouping the information – not too many or few groups. [1] Appropriate for the chosen landscape. [1]

10. True [1]

11. River B flows faster. [1]
    Explanation: Because its channel is smoother/channel of river A is rougher [1], so water has to overcome the friction [1], which uses energy so speed/velocity reduces.

12. Pakistan [1]

13. a) Answer needs to convey 'barrenness'. Could suggest that for much of the time there is no/almost no visible vegetation. [1] No trees can grow at all. [1] Limited opportunity for plant growth. [1] The landscape is often windswept [1], with very thin/no soil/soil which is frozen for much of the year giving a bleak appearance. [1] **[Any two points or one developed idea up to a maximum of 2 marks]**

    b) Few species [1]; generally slow growing [1]; small [1]; drought resistant [1]; cold tolerant [1]; often red-coloured leaves. [1] **[Any two points up to a maximum of 2 marks]**

    c) Larger animals, mainly herbivores, e.g. reindeer, migrate to warmer places in winter but move back as soon as temperatures rise enough for rapid plant growth. Some smaller mammals might hibernate. Coats change colour to white for camouflage, e.g. Arctic hare and fox. Birds also migrate, returning to Tundra to feed on huge summer insect populations. **[1 mark for naming species (name of species alone will not receive the mark), up to 4 marks for two explained ideas or four individual points]**

14. North Korea, Thailand, Singapore, Vietnam [1]

15. a) Number of people who might be affected for emergency planning/scale of planning needed. [1]

    b) This is about the vulnerability of a place and its population. Communications types/efficiency [1]; Emergency facilities [1]; Age groups; economy/whether principally farming etc. [1] Any reasonable ideas.

16. Everest [1]

17. Could be a number of ideas covered. 2 marks will be given for a theme and explanation, e.g. Quarrying for building material might involve blasting which creates noise and/or dust. [2] Cutting of quarries or mines can destabilise ground leading to subsidence/landslides. [2] Some extraction uses a lot of water which could affect the supplies in the area/water table and possibly pollute water courses. [2] Visual pollution/damage to vegetation might be quoted. **[Maximum of 4 marks available]**

18. Poland; Romania; Czech Republic [3]

19. a) Crater [1]
    b) Secondary cone [1]
    c) Crater lake [1]
    d) Volcano not erupted for long time [1], pressure built up/very violent eruption [1], which blows off the top of the volcano. [1]

20.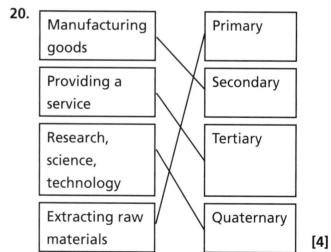
    [4]

21. a) Multi-sided/three or more sided shape which delimits/creates boundaries of a particular feature. [1]

b) Each shape idea could get 2 marks. The question asks for examples and explanation so a list, however big, cannot be credited. Examples: Rectangles for buildings **[1]**, combinations of rectangles for areas like shopping centres or housing estates **[1]** to show actual shape/footprint on the ground **[1]**; Irregular shapes to show natural features/lakes/mountain ranges **[1]** to show relationship of different features to each other **[1]**; Use of accurate/actual shape means measurements can be taken from the maps **[1]**, e.g. areas/perimeters/distances between, for analysis of patterns. **[1]** **[Suggest two [or more] shapes with reasons for 2 marks + 2 marks up to a maximum of 4 marks]**

22. Intermediate technology **[1]**
23. a) Swash **[1]**
    b) Backwash **[1]**
24. North Korea **[1]**
25. Disintegration is breaking up of solid rock **[1]** without change to its composition **[1]** whereas decomposition changes the rock itself **[1]** and creates new materials/allows minerals to be dissolved/breaking it down into materials which are more easily attacked or carried away. **[1]** Both processes must be considered **[for 2 marks]**, and the differences made clear **[for 2 marks, making a total of 4 marks]**.
26. Africa **[1]**
27.

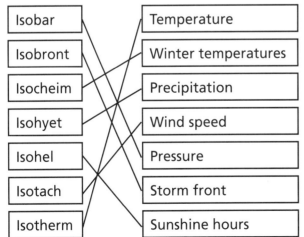

Isobar		Temperature
Isobront		Winter temperatures
Isocheim		Precipitation
Isohyet		Wind speed
Isohel		Pressure
Isotach		Storm front
Isotherm		Sunshine hours

[1 mark for each correct answer up to a maximum of 6 marks for seven correct answers]

28. Violent crime; Poor transport links; Unemployment **[3]**
29. a) 1:25000 maps show greater detail that would enable a walker to plan routes. **[1]** All footpaths/rights of way etc. are clearer/more comprehensive. **[1]**
    b) Slope/how much land rises in a given distance. **[1]**
    c)

[1 mark for each correct answer up to a maximum of 3 marks]

30. A squatter settlement where people do not own the land but build houses on it. **[1]**
31. Clay 25% **[1]**; Silt 65% **[1]**
32. a) Near total elimination of a life form/s. **[1]**
    b) Ice ages **[1]**
33. Rising/raised temperatures due to climate change **[1]**
34. High birth rate, high death rate, low life expectancy, high infant mortality **[1]**
35. Oil **[1]**

Acknowledgements

The authors and publisher are grateful to the copyright holders for permission to use quoted materials and images.

Pages 7, 9, 13, 15: Maps © Collins Bartholomew Ltd 2020

Page 18: River Niger in Kogi State Nigeria © Sani Ahmad Usman <https://commons.wikimedia.org/wiki/File:River_Niger_in_Kogi_state_Nigeria.jpg>. This file is licensed under the Creative Commons Attribution-Share Alike 4.0 International license <https://creativecommons.org/licenses/by-sa/4.0/deed.en>

Page 39: Paul Weston / Alamy Stock Photo

Page 52: The Brandt Line © Jovan.gec <https://commons.wikimedia.org/wiki/File:The_Brandt_Line.png>. This file is licensed under the Creative Commons Attribution-Share Alike 4.0 International license <https://creativecommons.org/licenses/by-sa/4.0/deed.en>

Page 56: World Map - Energy Use 2013 © Thomasjamc <https://commons.wikimedia.org/wiki/File:World_Map_-_Energy_Use_2013.png>. This file is licensed under the Creative Commons Attribution-Share Alike 4.0 International license <https://creativecommons.org/licenses/by-sa/4.0/deed.en>

Pages 63, 64: Maps use map data licensed from Ordnance Survey © Crown copyright and database rights (2016) Ordnance Survey (100018598)

Pages 66, 67: Maps produced by MAGIC on 17/07/2020. © Crown Copyright and database rights 2020. Ordnance Survey 100022861. Copyright resides with the data suppliers and the map must not be reproduced without their permission. Some information in MAGIC is a snapshot of information that is being maintained or continually updated by the originating organisation. Please refer to the documentation for details, as information may be illustrative or representative rather than definitive at this stage.

Page 67: © Crown Copyright. Contains public sector information licensed under the Open Government Licence v1.0

Page 71: productie van de afbeelding uit het .shp-bestand: Koenb at Dutch Wikipedia / Public domain

All other images ©Shutterstock.com and ©HarperCollinsPublishers

Every effort has been made to trace copyright holders and obtain their permission for the use of copyright material. The authors and publisher will gladly receive information enabling them to rectify any error or omission in subsequent editions. All facts are correct at time of going to press.

Published by Collins
An imprint of HarperCollins*Publishers*
1 London Bridge Street
London SE1 9GF

HarperCollins*Publishers*
Macken House, 39/40 Mayor Street Upper,
Dublin 1, D01 C9W8, Ireland

ISBN: 978-0-00-839992-4

First published 2020

10 9 8 7 6 5

© HarperCollins*Publishers* Ltd. 2020

British Library Cataloguing in Publication Data.

A CIP record of this book is available from the British Library.

Authors: Janet Hutson and Dan Major
Publisher: Katie Sergeant
Project Manager: Chantal Addy
Editorial: Jill Laidlaw
Cover Design: Kevin Robbins and Sarah Duxbury
Inside Concept Design: Sarah Duxbury, Paul Oates and Ian Wrigley
Text design and Layout: Jouve India Private Limited
Production: Karen Nulty
Printed in Great Britain by Martins the Printers

MIX
Paper | Supporting responsible forestry
FSC™ C007454

This book is produced from independently certified FSC™ paper to ensure responsible forest management.

For more information visit:
www.harpercollins.co.uk/green